The Art of Becoming

The Art of Becoming

How Group Improvisation Works

RAYMOND A. R. MACDONALD
AND GRAEME B. WILSON

OXFORD
UNIVERSITY PRESS

Oxford University Press is a department of the University of Oxford. It furthers the University's objective of excellence in research, scholarship, and education by publishing worldwide. Oxford is a registered trade mark of Oxford University Press in the UK and certain other countries.

Published in the United States of America by Oxford University Press
198 Madison Avenue, New York, NY 10016, United States of America.

Library of Congress Cataloging-in-Publication Data
Names: MacDonald, Raymond A. R. author. | Wilson, Graeme B. author.
Title: The art of becoming : how group improvisation works /
Raymond A. R. MacDonald, Graeme B. Wilson.
Description: New York : Oxford University Press, 2020. |
Includes bibliographical references and index.
Identifiers: LCCN 2019042456 (print) | LCCN 2019042457 (ebook) |
ISBN 9780190840914 (hardback) | ISBN 9780190840921 (paperback) |
ISBN 9780190840945 (epub) | ISBN 9780190840952
Subjects: LCSH: Improvisation (Music) |
Improvisation (Music)—Psychological aspects. |
Improvisation (Music)—Social aspects.
Classification: LCC MT68 .M116 2020 (print) | LCC MT68 (ebook) |
DDC 781.3/6—dc23
LC record available at https://lccn.loc.gov/2019042456
LC ebook record available at https://lccn.loc.gov/2019042457

Contents

Foreword: On the *Art of Becoming*

George E. Lewis

Written by two major figures in the fields of music and music psychology, this book is an important new articulation in the metafield of critical improvisation studies, which has exploded in recent years with a surge in interdisciplinary inquiry across many artistic and nominally non-artistic fields. The rich panoply of fields in the arts, humanities, and the social and natural sciences that have been enriched by the improvisative turn include anthropology and sociology; organisational, political, cognitive, and computer science; musicology, ethnomusicology, performance studies, dance, film, poetry, theatre, and new media; economics, theology, neuroscience, and psychology; philosophy, cultural studies, literary theory, and classics; gender and sexuality studies; architecture and urban planning; science and technology studies; education; and many others.

In fact, improvisation is everywhere, but it can be very hard to see—because this ubiquitous practice of innovation in everyday life, fundamental to the existence and survival of every human formation, is as close to universal as contemporary critical method could responsibly entertain. This book makes an important contribution to the visibility of the practice, by ringingly asserting music's leading role in social-scientific work and showing that the scientific study of musical improvisation provides us with new understandings of the human condition.

The uniqueness of this volume is due in considerable measure to the fact that its authors, Raymond MacDonald and Graeme Wilson, have distinguished themselves at the highest levels in multiple areas—as social scientists, as pedagogues, and as practitioners of the musical art of improvisation. Their integral artist-scholar-teacher identity enables MacDonald and Wilson to combine artistic research on musical improvisation with insights and methods from psychology in ways that encourage the two domains to inform each other. Here, Wilson and MacDonald are using their introspective experience as improvisors to develop scientific insights on musical improvisation, while in turn deploying those insights to illuminate both theoretical and practical understandings of the practice.

The authors interrogate a number of clichés about musical improvisation, often enough expressed as baleful binaries. These include the process-product opposition, where musical improvisors are said to be vastly more concerned with the former. MacDonald and Wilson, along with the musicians they engage as research informants, assert the importance of considering the interaction between both. The authors also give refreshingly short shrift to the common imputation regarding musical improvisation's ostensibly inherent and inevitable "constraints." This trope, one suspects, emerges from the binary opposition between improvisation and composition found in earlier classical music histories and criticism, where "real-time" too often becomes characterised as "time-bound," in distinction to composition's putative freedom from the tyranny of the temporal.

Discussions of constraint have suffered from a discourse that frames constraints as somehow outside of the system of improvisative production itself, quickly morphing from an initial presumption of the presence of constraints in any musical improvisation process (and product) to a final assertion of a fundamental need for constraint as a precondition for any "successful" musical improvisation.

The latter assertion can appear aggressively bereft of corroboration. For example, in his important 1964 book on the anthropology of music, Alan Merriam admitted, "While it is clear that there must always be limits imposed upon improvisation, we do not know what these limits are" (Merriam, 1964, 179). The standard view tends to portray constraint as a kind of prison with already defined borders (see Pickering, 1995). One gleans from such theories the sense of a deeply rooted fear that musical improvisation, like noise, slaves, or subjects of authoritarian regimes, can easily get out of hand and run buck wild, overturning "good order." Rather than obsessing over constraints, or the related mapping of freedom-structure and improvisation-composition binaries onto low/high culture opposition, Wilson and MacDonald emphasise the freedoms of identity and social interaction that musical improvisation offers, where structure and freedom—as well as power, agency, and constraint—become emergent in the musical interaction.

At one point, the authors pose the question: "How can improvisation be explicable yet unfathomable, intellectual yet instinctual, specialist yet amateur, traditional yet unfettered by expectations?" I'd like to suggest that these additional binaries emerge from the interface between musical improvisation and the worlds of musical genre. They recall the demands frequently made of musical improvisation that the best of it will be "unique, avoid stagnation and the commonplace, and constantly display or embody innovation, originality (albeit via recombination of existing elements), novelty, freshness, and surprise" (Lewis and Piekut, 2016, 11). While some of these criteria are regularly applied to artistic production in general, the time-based yardsticks take on special meaning when musical improvisation is considered.

This work builds on pioneering research on musical identities by MacDonald, David Hargreaves, and Dorothy Miell (2017, 2002), who have identified the powerful effects of music on personality, values, and well-being. In this book, MacDonald and Wilson present musical improvisation as a central practice of identity formation and maintenance that is socially as well as individually performed, and productive of larger musical scenes. The by-now ubiquitous curatorial practice asserted by guitarist Derek Bailey in his various "Company" formulations, in which musicians who were often not previously acquainted with each other, and who were bearers of diverse identities domains of gender, race, sexuality, class, and aesthetics, exploited both interpersonal dynamics and cultural difference (Bailey, 1993, 133ff.). Here, musical identities coalesce to draw the outlines of what I have termed a "social location" (Lewis, 1996, 110) a site for working out musical identities.

Remarkably, the authors extend their understanding of musical identities to include machine identities, expressed in social interaction as musical identities must be. Interactive computer music has drawn upon theories of artificial intelligence and practices of free improvisation in creating a new kind of music making that includes machine subjectivities as central actors. What I have called "creative machines" stake out musical territory, assess and respond to conditions, and assert identities and positions—all aspects of improvisative interaction, both within and beyond the domain of music. Relations among people and interactive systems constitute hybrid socialities, a notion I draw from composer-theorist Rich Gold's pioneering essays on ubiquitous computing, which led to today's understanding of an "Internet of Things" (Lewis, 2017).

Particularly in earlier jazz studies literature, the identity of the artist was often deemed homologous with the musical results, leading quickly to the invocation of notions of genius and self-expression that the authors pointedly avoid. Rather than allowing the image of musical improvisation (or for that matter, creativity itself) to be colonised and commodified as the exclusive and ineffable domain of designated superpeople with powers and abilities far beyond those of mere mortals, MacDonald and Wilson present musical improvisation as an inherently open-access practice at a human scale, "a social and universally accessible form of collaborative creativity." Indeed, on this basis one could even conclude that creativity itself is inherently improvisative; if so, creativity becomes a human birthright.

Musical improvisation's apparent unrepeatability and resistance to codification has often been identified with an imputation of ephemerality, and as a result, the practice has been portrayed as necessarily devoid of method. Earlier generations of jazz-identified musicians produced theoretical treatises designed in part to refute that notion. The most famous of these is the late composer-pianist George Russell's 1953 *Lydian Chromatic Concept of Tonal Organization*, a fearsomely complex combination of harmonic theory and musical ideology that both composers and improvisors used to create unusual harmonic complexes. Russell's book and its many offshoots and successors benefited from an emphasis on harmony as a codifiable aspect of equal temperament that rendered traditional forms of jazz amenable to already established techniques for thinking about method and analysis in classical music.

That codification began to break down with the advent of free jazz and free improvisation in the early 1960s, and a recent book by the improvisor-guitarist Joe Morris, *Perpetual Frontier: The Properties of Free Music*, examines systems through which improvisors create their work (Morris, 2012, 1). Morris seeks to describe "the reconfiguring and repurposing of properties that are constantly in play in a large body of music that, by practice, seeks to avoid a final and codified explanation." Attempts to repurpose earlier methodologies yielded little understanding about what Morris calls "free music"; at the same time, while the absence of codified musical features made free music attractive to a newer generation of creative musicians, only a few treatises have been published on method in free improvisation or its various offshoots and tributaries (see Dean, 1989 for a particularly salutary early contribution).

Morris explicitly addresses the lack of any defining method, system, or feature of free music by providing a smorgasbord of possibilities designed to show that no technique or method can be alien to the genre. Indeed, many of the author's examples of musical method are borrowed from other genres of music, including composed music. This contributes to a framing of free music as something of a hybrid, an aspect of musical improvisation that

MacDonald and Wilson take as a starting point for their own hybrid work. It is the connection with experimentalism itself that allows these hybrid scientist-artists to take on the challenge of somehow codifying the uncodifiable and thinking about the unthinkable. Indeed, Wilson and MacDonald's claim is that an *experimental* attitude provides a frame that clarifies the issues at stake in understanding how musical improvisation works.

In this book, scientific inquiry and artistic experience provide mutual underpinnings, and the experimentalism of musical method promulgated by MacDonald and Wilson is complimented by their design of experiments that focus in on what is truly important about the experience and practice of musical improvisation. Their production of experimental evidence in the form of qualitative studies that include actual improvised music making lead to their intriguing effort to promulgate an actual methodology for musical free improvisation, based on an experiment in which a set of what might be called "focus groups" of improvisors created and discussed their own short improvisations, with the aim of moving to illuminate the nature of decision making and negotiation. MacDonald and Wilson then organised performances based on their findings as to the criteria their focus groups identified as salient to decision making in musical improvisation.

Five key improvisative strategies—initiating, maintaining, adopting, augmenting, and contrasting—provided the substrate for a performances of a new work, *Stones, Clouds*, in which improvisors consciously deployed these model-based strategies as real-time generators of improvisations. Here, the authors are not so much defining musical improvisation as describing and testing their understanding of some key features of the practice, some of which amount to a form of practical relational aesthetics. The authors' description of "conscious decisions" to assert these kinds of positionalities amounts to a kind of methodology based in musical free improvisation itself, rather than borrowed from other musical genres.

Here, I would like to augment the authors' discussion of virtuosity to address the understanding of the Scottish improvisor-vocalist Maggie Nicols, one of the founding mothers of free improvisation in Europe, that musical improvisors deploy "social virtuosity—social skills really," involving "how you are in the community . . . Being able to have that kind of creative spontaneity in every aspect of your life" (quoted in Smith, 2004, 236). In that light, I would like to experiment in this foreword with bringing the theory of musical identities together with Georgina Born's theoretical framework of musical mediation, within which she has identified four distinct yet overlapping planes (Born, 2017).

In the first plane, "music produces its own diverse socialities—in the immediate microsocialities of musical performance and practice and in the social relations embodied in musical ensembles and associations" (Born, 2017, 43). Born identifies this first plane as characteristic of the performing arts, and to be sure, the research of Wilson and MacDonald has produced ample experimental corroboration for the production of microsocialties within musical improvisation.

I want to suggest that it is on planes two and three of Born's theory that musical identities reside, with musical improvisation providing an agentic tool for imagining and enacting community. In Born's second plane, "music has powers to animate imagined communities, aggregating its listeners into affective alliances, virtual collectivities or publics based on musical and other identifications" (43). Born's third plane also recalls musical identities, in the sense that "music refracts wider social relations . . . music's instantiation of the nation, of social hierarchies, or of the social relations of class, race, religion, ethnicity, gender, or sexuality" (43). Similarly, for MacDonald and Wilson, musical improvisation "transcends musical genres and facilitates collaboration," encompassing both shared and unshared understandings, conversations, musical tastes, education, family environment, and affinity and friendship groupings. Indeed, "community music" is a vital concern of this book.

In Born's fourth plane, musical improvisation becomes a central staging ground for asserting music's place in "the broader institutional forces that provide the basis for its production, reproduction, and transformation, whether elite or religious patronage, market or non-market exchange, public and subsidized cultural institutions, or late capitalism's multi-polar cultural economy" (43). Analogously, as MacDonald and Wilson observe, the kinds of experimental musical improvisation they are studying and performing "intersects with experimental approaches to artistic practice to foster new work that often tackles issues of politics, gender, race, economics, environment, community etc.," as well as being researched at every level of educational institution.

MacDonald and Wilson's model of improvisation features five key, defining elements: improvisation is *creative, social, ambiguous, spontaneous*, and *accessible*. To my mind, these characteristics constitute not so much a definition of musical improvisation as components of a situated social aesthetic. Moreover, any attempt to define improvisation as a whole, or even musical improvisation, would need to take into account the fact that important discussions of improvisation have been taking place in a number of fields that have little or no investment in musical histories and ideologies.

For instance, even as MacDonald and Wilson identify negotiation as an important aspect of musical improvisation, two scholars in organisational science, Kathleen McGinn and Angela Keros, portrayed the practice of negotiation in business settings as "a coherent sequence of relational, informational, and procedural actions and responses created, chosen, and carried out by the parties during the social interaction" (McGinn and Keros, 2002, 445). The prosaic and provisional nature of this definition, which expands the frame of reference beyond the artistic, places considerable pressure on ideologies that impose upon the concept of musical improvisation the special sense of creative autonomy and uniqueness that so many commentators on music portray as fundamental.

Considering literary scholar Fred Moten's observation about "the very intense relationship between experimentalism and the everyday" (Rowell, 2004, 965, quoted in Piekut, 2011, 1), it comes as no surprise that Wilson and MacDonald find a crucial connection between improvisation as being-in-the-world and the quotidian: "Each time we take a walk we need to decide afresh how to negotiate other pedestrians, when to cross the road, when to stop and chat to an acquaintance and when to finish the conversation and move on." Moreover, improvisation for MacDonald and Wilson is not only quotidian, but primordial: "Improvisation plays an important role in the earliest and most important bonding relationships of our lives. We can improvise before we talk."

Another vital concern of these scientist-scholars is collective responsibility, to which, the authors maintain, notions of freedom and of individualism are explicitly linked. Collective responsibility is reasserted throughout this book as an ethical concern that produces artistic effects, and rather than summarising the authors' ideas, I want to place these ideas in dialogue with the work of the philosopher Arnold I. Davidson on musical improvisation with computers. Commenting in a panel discussion on pianist Alexander von Schlippenbach's 2010 performance with my computer program *Voyager* (Lewis, 2000), Davidson observes that computer interactivity exemplifies the desire for social responsibility:

> *When you try to respond to someone, being responsible to them, to that particular person, one of the ways you tell is how they then respond to you. So when you hear the way they're playing, I think you see a very clear aspect of interactive responsibility, the social dimension of responsibility. Part of the response is not doing anything, because often or sometimes social responsibility is expressed by letting the other person have their say. And it seemed to me that in the*

> *piece here, all of those aspects of social responsibility—trying to respond to what it [the computer] was doing, letting it have its say, sometimes trying to influence what it would say—which is part of responsibility as well. When you think it might not be doing so well, you want to do something that helps it along. And you'd hope that someone would help you along.* (quoted in Lewis, 2019, 441–42)

Davidson connects social responsibility with collective intelligibility, which "unfolds in real time when the participants in social interaction are committed to making sense of, and giving sense to, themselves and others" (quoted in Lewis, 2019, 444). Analogously to McGinn and Keros, MacDonald and Wilson take issue with the idea that shared understanding between musical improvisers constitutes a necessary precondition for success. Rather, joint investment in the process is vital, leading to the possibility that intelligibility is constructed by the participants in real time, further mediated by participation in larger scenes over time.

Another link between Davidson's thought and the work of Wilson and MacDonald lies in the former's framing of "improvisation as a way of life" that encourages us to "disrupt our fixed framework and introduce creativity, where previously we were restrained by habit." This concern, which is both ethical and practical, recalls Gilbert Ryle's "Improvisation" (1976), an essay that never mentions music, with its resounding declaration that if the normal human "is not at once *improvising* and improvising *warily*, he is not engaging his somewhat trained wits in some momentarily live issue, but perhaps acting from sheer unthinking habit" (Ryle, 1976, 77).

Davidson has declared that "We have to detach ourselves from the already given systems, orders, doctrines, and codes of philosophy" to open out to "a new ethos of spiritual change" (quoted in Lewis, 2019, 437). In that light, the kinds of experimental work MacDonald and Wilson are both studying and performing is often aimed at just this type of interrogation and disruption of the unexamined life. I believe that the authors would fully endorse

Davidson's declaration that "improvisation must fully become an experimental work on what is presented to us as our natural or inevitable limits" (quoted in Lewis, 2019, 437).

The issue of "freedom" is ever-present in discussion of "free" musical improvisation. In Davidson's conception, "The space of liberty is up to us," where freedom itself emerges from an improvisative life in which "self-transformation, intertwined with social formation, will occupy the centre of our ethical and political work." In such a life, Davidson warns us, "nothing is guaranteed . . . Each of us must decide if this ethos is worth the trouble and the risk" (quoted in Lewis, 2019, 440–441).

Davidson's model of the care and transformation of the self has strong resonances with the ways in which the authors build on the work of specialists in well-being and pedagogy, such as Émile Jaques-Dalcroze, Fritz Hegi, Tony Wigram, Tia DeNora, and Patricia Shehan Campbell, as well as their own innovative work. Wilson and MacDonald review and extend the area of music therapy as an ongoing site for innovation in using musical improvisation to promote and maintain well-being, ameliorating pain and dementia, overcoming learning and communication difficulties, and simply helping people to get along in the world. Or, as Arnold Davidson once quoted Lester Bowie simply, "Artists teach people how to live."

MacDonald and Wilson have provided the field with a rich array of possibilities for future research. Just as critical improvisation studies draw crucially but by no means exclusively from musical experience, many of the authors' findings make common cause with those of scholars working on improvisation in non-artistic domains, encouraging the widest range of interdisciplinary cross-fertilisation. The authors continually unearth discoveries that bear strong analogues with non-artistic fields—organisational science's research on negotiation, or computer science's moves to create autonomously functioning machines such as self-driving vehicles—demonstrating that these fields can draw much of value from the social-scientific study of music.

This openness to experience outside of music becomes important when considering the place of indeterminacy. For the authors, "*Indeterminacy* places agency, status, and power at the hands of the composer while *Improvisation* puts agency, power, and status in the hands of the performer." I would like to suggest that this view, which draws on the opposition between improvisation and composition, would not be generalisable outside of the ideological domains of music. While it is arguably still the case that, as the authors assert, "The hegemony of Western music, built up over centuries, certainly places composition at the top of a clear and unambiguous hierarchy," alternatives to this hierarchy are available, and those seeking a strong basis for change will actually find support in the research of Wilson and MacDonald.

As an alternative, I would like to suggest that there is a role for indeterminacy here—not within or against improvisation, but fundamentally bound up with it. If, borrowing a conceit of David Harvey's, we can speak of a fundamental "condition" of improvisation, in my own conception of that condition, we are all agents, operating in a fundamental and continuous condition of indeterminacy, where we cannot fully know what will happen next; we analyse our environment for clues as to where we are and to seed judgements as to where we are headed—an activity which is itself improvised in that same condition; and finally, we make a choice. Before or after we make that choice, we can imagine it as proceeding from the analysis of the environment. However, we cannot be certain of either causality or correlation.

Perhaps I have set a very low bar for ascertaining the presence of improvisation. On the other hand, I would like to claim that the above elements—indeterminacy, agency, analysis, judgment, and choice—will be found in any improvised act whatsoever, artistic or not, by machines, humans, animals, etc. I would also like to suggest that these characteristics are sufficiently originary that in a given proceeding, the absence of any one of them means that the activity in question is not improvised.

This framework for recognising (if not defining) improvisation proceeds from the understanding that even as we continue to explore the nature and practice of musical improvisation, maintaining the coherence of our ideas beyond the frame of music calls for a certain vigilance in guarding the freedom of the concept of improvisation from possible colonisation by musical and artistic models. In maintaining that vigilance, we allow the invocation of both the personal and the social on a broader basis, while allowing a cross-pollination between music and the wider world in which we can understand indeterminacy as an aspect of everyday life that is addressed improvisatively. Right along with Raymond MacDonald and Graeme Wilson, we can celebrate an *Art of Becoming* as achievement without attainment: like modernity, an incomplete, yet open-ended project.

Preface

A Dancing Star

> One must still have chaos in oneself to be able to give birth to a dancing star.
>
> —Friedrich Nietzsche[1]

Nietzsche recognised the centrality of the unpredictable, of "chaos" in his particular passion of dance. A proponent of the arts, Nietzsche danced daily, saying it was his "only kind of piety," his "divine service." This was partly due to his belief in "life-affirmation" through artistic pursuits and the questioning of all activities that drain life's vast but finite energy from us; a day to him was lost if it did not involve dance. A century on from Nietzsche's enthusiasm for improvisation, there is no doubt that this practice is enjoying a particular renaissance. This book appears at a time when there is unprecedented global interest in improvisation within all branches of the arts, and is partly motivated by the excitement generated by this teeming upsurge in spontaneous creativity.

Another motivation for this book comes from a series of empirical studies we have undertaken over the past fifteen years. This began with two small focus groups in 2004 when we worked together at Glasgow Caledonian University. These focus groups brought together professional jazz musicians working in Scotland,

[1] Friedrich Nietzsche (1883) *Thus Spake Zarathustra*, prologue, sec. 5 (tr. Walter Kaufmann).

all of whom were acquaintances. We wanted to ask them how they went about improvising; what struck us in their talk was the impassioned views they expressed about their life in music, and the careful negotiations that emerged to reach an agreed account of how they played, both of which seemed psychologically important. This motivated further research where we interviewed diverse musicians about their life and improvisational practices, and eventually about improvisations that had just taken place. This qualitative work led to the development of a model that we propose as the mechanism of group improvisation in all non-verbal performance arts. We feel that now is a good time to synthesise and develop these key findings, propose some overarching themes, and point the way forward for future research.

A third motivating factor in developing this work was our track record together as musicians. We began collaborating over thirty years ago as a busking saxophone duo called *Cast of 1000s* playing on the streets of Glasgow, graduating to the streets of Amsterdam and beyond. Cast of 1000s grew into in a saxophone quartet, *The Hung Drawn Quartet*, with whom we played in jazz venues, airports, swimming pools, car showrooms, shopping centres, and a football stadium, and on boats, trains, buses, skyscraper rooftops, and on top of a sixty-foot Christmas tree. Performing with dancers, filmmakers, and artists, we began exploring how to engage with artists in other media. In 2002 we were both founding members of *Glasgow Improvisers Orchestra*, a large ensemble pulling together musicians from different genres to explore new ways of improvising. Forging a collaborative practice in both improvised performance and research has given us the desire to produce a text that is grounded in our academic work but crucially informed by our performing together as musicians over the past decades. Working together as musicians has helped shape our approach to theory, methods, and research overall. We recognise the importance of understanding how musicians talk about their music, their identities, and their improvisation; partly because of our own experience touring, recording, and performing, and through those experiences observing how the stories of improvisers merge with their practice. We believe that improvisation represents a primary mode of creative interaction for collective performance, but at the same time a fundamental process though which identities are negotiated. Talk about improvising determines how improvisers perform and vice versa; improvisation therefore has to be understood as a component of the lives devoted to it.

The final motivating factor in producing the text has been chief commissioning editor at Oxford University Press, Suzanne Ryan. Suzanne's advice, encouragement, insights, and all-round good humour have been vital in getting this book not only off the ground but firmly into orbit, and we would like to thank her warmly and sincerely for her inspirational help. We would also very much like to thank our partners and families, Tracy Ibbotson, Cath Keay, Nadia MacDonald, Maria MacDonald, and Eva MacDonald for their endless and ongoing support, patience, and advice. We are also immensely grateful to all the improvisers who gave their time, creativity, and thoughts to our research. Without their generous input this book and our ideas would be impossible. Finally, we would like to think our friend and inspirational polymath, George Lewis, for generously and expertly providing the Foreword. We hope you enjoy reading this book as much as we have enjoyed writing it. While around the globe we are living through turbulent times, whatever the future holds for us, it will be improvised.

Raymond MacDonald
Graeme Wilson

1
Improvisation and new frontiers in creative practice

Improvisation is a creative practice whose time has come. This social and universally accessible form of collaborative creativity continues to flourish in underground and mainstream music making around the world and is studied in universities and conservatoires globally. It transcends musical genres and facilitates collaboration between practitioners from disciplines across the artistic spectrum. A steady growth in interest may not be matched with economic rewards, but most cities around the world are home to at least a small and vibrant scene of performers who will define themselves with reference to their use of improvisation; while many cities host effervescent intergenerational communities of musicians who explore the creative possibilities of improvisation as a primary means of musical expression.

Improvisation is a fundamental aspect of life. The earliest communication between a parent and a child is musical and improvisatory. The interactions between a newborn baby and parents are rhythmic, melodic, and essentially an improvised and interactive song unfolding in real time. These improvisatory patterns of interaction that occur in the early weeks and months will help shape a child's developing personality and will therefore be influential across an individual's lifespan. Thus, improvisation plays an important role in the earliest and most important bonding relationships of our lives. We can improvise before we can talk.

The ebb and flow of daily behaviour is governed by a series of decisions that also require us to be very good improvisers. Each

The Art of Becoming. Raymond A. R. MacDonald and Graeme B. Wilson, Oxford University Press (2020).

DOI: 10.1093/oso/9780190840914.001.0001

time we take a walk we need to decide afresh how to negotiate other pedestrians, when to cross the road, when to stop and chat to an acquaintance, and when to finish the conversation and move on. Because situations never recur in exactly the same way, these decisions all have improvisation at their heart, and so we are all improvising on many levels simultaneously. The ubiquitous presence of improvisation was acknowledged by Gilbert Ryle, the British empiricist philosopher, who stated that "a brain that is not improvising is not alive" (Ryle, 1949).

Improvisation is also an essential clinical process, utilised by therapists to develop beneficial relationships with others through music. As a distinct channel of communication, musical improvisation can help develop healing relationships. While this book focuses primarily on music, we will make many links to other areas highlighting some commonalities for improvisation across disciplines and contexts.

In this opening chapter we outline some of the ways in which improvisation plays an important role within contemporary music making and other selected areas. This is not intended as an exhaustive survey of the global landscape of improvisatory practice, rather we select some examples to highlight how improvisation is an important social and creative process. The examples demonstrate ways in which improvisation is increasingly embraced as a dynamic approach to creating new artistic works and generating conceptual breakthroughs.

From the edges to the mainstream

Over the last twenty years the visibility of improvised music as an innovative and vibrant way of creating new work has grown immeasurably at festivals and venues around the world. Many events now have improvisation as a defining feature. This allows programmers, musicians, and other practitioners to present new work that is not tied to a genre of music or even a particular art form, but rather uses spontaneous and collaborative artistic interaction as a way of developing new work and engaging with the public on many levels. Improvisation also resonates strongly with the concept of *post-genre* music making where the boundaries between different types of music become blurred, purposively ignored, or completely removed. Improvisation intersects with experimental approaches to artistic practice to foster new work that often tackles issues of politics, gender, race, economics, environment, community, etc. The proliferation and growth of these festivals is evidence that improvisation, as a creative practice that fosters collaboration and cross-disciplinary work, is going from strength to strength. The following are some examples of international festivals that have improvisational practice as a defining feature:

- The *Now Now Festival* of spontaneous music, experimental sound, and outlier performance has been presented annually since 2001 in Sydney, Australia. It is a musician-run event that features Australian and international artists, musicians, dancers, and sound artists performing and collaborating.[1]
- In Lebanon, the Irtijal festival was founded in 2001 by musicians Mazen Kerbaj and Sharif Sehnaoui and lays claim to being the oldest music festival in Beirut. With a programme including experimental music, free jazz, free improvisation, contemporary music, noise, and free rock, it attracts musicians from around the world and is focused upon experimental music making, with improvisation as a key element.[2]
- Running annually since 2002, *All Ears* is a Norwegian festival in Oslo for improvisation in music and related art forms.

[1] http://www.thenownow.net.
[2] http://irtijal.org/irtijal/irtijal-2017-overview/.

Recent festivals have included an improvised concert in a sauna and an overnight "sleeping concert."[3]

- The Guelph jazz festival in Canada, founded in 1994, is a music festival that explores new approaches to improvisation and cross-disciplinary work with an explicit remit to engage with the wider social, cultural, and psychological issues around improvisation.[4]
- In Scotland, Glasgow Improvisers Orchestra run an international festival of improvisation focusing on large ensemble improvisation. Running annually since 2007 the festival includes cross-disciplinary performances and workshops for young children and members of the public.[5]

In addition to festivals there are a number of international societies exploring improvisation in cross-disciplinary contemporary contexts. The International Society for Improvised Music has a focus on how improvisation can foster new insights into creativity across different fields including music, dance, film, and visual art. They have specific interests in research, education, and cross-cultural approaches to improvisation.[6]

Events where organisers attempt to push aesthetic and conceptual boundaries and cross genres are not new; Dadaist, Fluxus, and "The Happenings" scenes from across the twentieth century all share some of these features. However, earlier movements challenged norms by being shocking and visibly oppositional (Monson, 2007; Ross, 2009). Contrastingly, contemporary festivals, while often still retaining radical artistic and political agendas, are less focused on creating outrage and shock. Contemporary festivals and events tend to emphasise improvisation, with music as a focus, as a means of fostering collaboration or an exciting way of presenting

[3] https://www.all-ears.no
[4] https://guelphjazzfestival.com
[5] https://glasgowimprovisersorchestra.com
[6] http://www.improvisedmusic.org

new work, rather than provocation. Improvisation is clearly moving out of the cultural shadows and more into the mainstream. A recent text by Corbett (2016) presents a listener's guide to free improvisation highlighting key features but importantly emphasising its accessibility for all listeners.

The growth of improvisation courses in universities and conservatoires around the world means students can complete higher education with a well-developed set of improvisatory skills and experiences. These skills can be used to help build careers, foster collaborative artistic relationships, and facilitate creative development. Many prestigious institutions such as The Estonian Academy of Music and Mills College in San Francisco combine teaching in improvisation with experimental composition and performance techniques to offer qualifications that have improvisation as a defining feature. Figure 1.1 shows an ingenious new game for

Figure 1.1 "Improvopoly," by Holly Carmichael. An example of student work from the undergraduate course "Improvisation as Social Process" at the University of Edinburgh

improvisers developed by Holly Carmichael during her studies in Edinburgh.

Also in the United States, recent recipients of the prestigious MacArthur Fellowships for individuals who have shown "extraordinary originality and dedication in their creative pursuits and a marked capacity for self-direction" have included: George Lewis (2002), Regina Carter (2006), Jason Moran (2010), Vijay Iyer (2013), Steve Coleman (2014), Tyshawn Sorey (2017), Okwui Okpokwasili (2018), and Mary Halvorson (2019). These are all musicians who work extensively in improvisation.[7] These examples demonstrate a growing level of institutional recognition for improvisation and evidence of how improvisation has become accepted as a legitimate field of study within higher education and a possible focus for building a career. There are clear signals that improvisation is moving from the margins of music into the mainstream of contemporary culture.

Features of contemporary improvising

In the following section we highlight how new technologies, new performance spaces, increases in cross-disciplinary working, and large ensemble improvisation are all key aspects of contemporary improvisatory practice.

New technologies

Technological advances have fundamentally alerted how we perform, listen to, and engage with music, and technology is a key influence on innovation in improvisation. This is particularly evident when we think of how new technologies have influenced

[7] https://www.macfound.org/programs/fellows/strategy/.

improvisational practices. Musicians improvise differently as a result of new technologies, and they also perform on new and nonconventional instruments. Computers can improvise unaided by human hands, and new technology gives access to improvisation and music making to people who have not had the opportunity to explore their creativity through music.

People interact differently

The revolution in music technology over the past thirty years has changed not only how we perform and consume music but also how people improvise. Developments in computer software technologies now facilitate real time sophisticated recording and playback. These recorded events can be immediately manipulated and incorporated into a performance context. Pioneering saxophonist Evan Parker's Electro Acoustic Ensemble's recordings for ECM are a good example of computers and technology facilitating developments in improvisational practices. Musicians such as Lawrence Casserley, Joel Ryan, and Adam Linson are given free rein to record specific elements of a performance which are manipulated and reintroduced into the ongoing performance.[8] Thus, performing musicians are not only playing conventional instruments but also using computer technology to develop new approaches to improvisational practices. American composer and accordionist Pauline Oliveros uniquely combined minimalist ideas with new technologies and a profound commitment to listening practices to produce an approach to improvisation that led to the founding of The Centre for Deep Listening.[9] A new generation of improvisers/composer/performers are using innovative technologies to develop performance practices and improvisation techniques. For example,

[8] Drawn inward, ECM 1693. The Evan Parker Electro-Acoustic Ensemble, 1999.
[9] http://deeplistening.org/

Lauren Hayes explored the relationship between new technologies, improvisation, and body movement to develop a new series of compositional and performance strategies (Hayes, 2017).

New kinds of improvisers

The rapid development in digital and computer technology has also helped produce a new generation of musicians who approach their practice in unique ways. Working with improvisation and technology is not necessarily new; groups such as AMM, and Music Improvisation Company were experimenting with improvisation and electronic technology from the mid-1960s. Richard Teitelbaum, from the pioneering improvising group Musica Elettronica Viva used electrical impulses generated by his brain to control the output of an early Moog Synthesizer in 1967 (Toop, 2016). However, today's virtuoso coders, software engineers, and algorithmic composers are exploring improvisation through technological innovations that are changing how we perform and collaborate with computers. The software of Edinburgh-based musician Martin Parker's computer piece *GruntCount* is designed to interact unpredictably in collaboration with a musician presenting new unique performance opportunities.[10] Developments in internet technology have facilitated real time collaborations between musicians in different physical locations. However, until recently, the time delay between a musician performing in one location and the musical gestures being received by musicians in another location had been so great that working together in real time across the internet was extremely challenging. New technology allows for near instant transmission of sounds and images across the internet. A ground-breaking project at Plymouth University (UK), for instance, facilitates remote improvising by using videoconferencing

[10] https://www.research.ed.ac.uk/portal/files/4091746/GruntCount.pdf

software to reduce network latency (the time delay from signal transmission to reception) over a standard broadband connection (Rofe & Geelhoed, 2017).[11] Another, LoLa, is a low latency, high quality audio/video transmission system for networking musical performances and interaction developed by Giuseppe Tartini at The Conservatorio di Musica in Italy, which enables musicians to collaborate and perform in real time via the internet.

Computers can improvise

Another way in which technology has contributed to advances in improvisation practice is in the development of software that can automatically produce improvisation. One of the first examples of this was a computer software programme, *Voyager*, developed by composer and musicologist George Lewis (Lewis, 2000) (Figure 3.1). Musicians improvise and the software facilitates computer responses by contributing musical improvisations to the ongoing performance unaided by another musician. Thus, new spontaneously composed music is being produced by a computer with no human involvement and the computer can be said to be improvising. In one particular example Lewis and German improvising pianist Alexander von Shlippenbach perform with this software as part of a public lecture. Following the performance Lewis and von Schlippenbach discuss at length the processes and outcomes of performing with a computer that generates improvised music in real time,[12] raising fundamental issues like how to begin a piece and how to end an improvisation while collaborating with the software. They agree that the biggest challenge for this software is knowing when the piece has ended. In this book we suggest these fundamental issues of choice during an improvisation are defining

[11] http://onlineorchestra.com/performance/
[12] https://www.youtube.com/watch?v=9r2JrwsGXFY.

elements of all improvising and chapters 4, 5, and 6 in this book provide detailed examples of how these choices are negotiated.

More people can access improvisation

New technology has given access to improvisational music making to people who otherwise may have been denied these opportunities. Technological advances, particularly those in digital technology, are also creating access to improvised music making without the need for conventional instruments. For example, The Skoog is an innovative digital instrument, a cube held in the hand that has been designed to be fully accessible especially to those unable to play conventional musical instruments. Its accessibility makes it particularly useful for music therapy, education and community music. It facilitates an improvisatory approach to music making since the instrument can produce a variety of sounds very quickly and with limited technical knowledge. Picking the cube up and gently turning it around can produce a sophisticated array of digital sounds depending upon how the instrument has been calibrated.[13]

New performance spaces

One recent advance in improvisational practice is the move to utilise unconventional performance spaces, to move beyond the concert hall or club venue to create work that intersects with sound art practices. This type of work is often termed *site specific*. The location plays a fundamental role in shaping the music as the players craft their performance in negotiation with the immediate environment. Japanese musician, inventor, instrument builder, and shaman Akio Suzuki's performances are characterised by a focus

[13] http://skoogmusic.com

on the improvisational moment in unconventional performance spaces and the sonic potential of unusual instruments such as stones and shells (Kennedy, 2013).

A performance location with a long reverberant echo, like a large cave with musicians inside the cave and audience outside, may provoke an improviser to use long tones punctured by periods of not playing while the cave creates a slowly decaying echo response. The following day in another location, a bandstand in a park, the acoustic properties of the performance space are different (less reverberant) and the audience surrounds the bandstand. The same improvisers may then produce a radically different performance with the musical material much denser and busier. Thus, the performance environment influences the musicians to create and improvise in new ways that could only be produced by the unique configuration of variables (the location, the musicians, the instrumentation, positioning and size of audience, etc.). The improvisation practices in these situations invite, and to some extent necessitate, the creation of a new performance space. The space becomes a negotiated space as audience and performers are not within a conventional performance venue. Therefore, some of the normal expectancies of how audience and performers interact are absent. There are no stalls or balcony or seat numbers or a conventional stage; it is a non-demarcated space that belongs equally to all collaborators. It could become a contested space as people figure out how to temporarily inhabit this environment and performers and audience each stake out their sonic and physical space. It is in this space that the new work is created and since it is not expected that the space will be replicated elsewhere, this new improvised work will be unique and unrepeatable. It will be contingent upon location, contingent upon collaborators, contingent upon available resources; indeed it will be contingent upon a huge array of factors that will render both the process of creation and the work created unique.

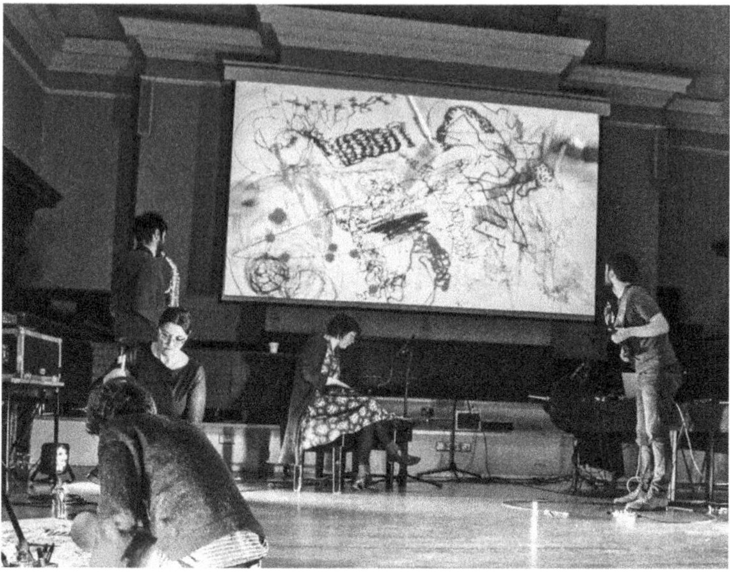

Figure 1.2 Artists Cath Keay and Simon Ortega and musicians Christian Ferlaino, Ceylan Hay, and Mike Parr-Burman improvising on stage together. Photo credit: Full Zoom Photography

Cross-disciplinary work

There has been an explosion of interest in cross-disciplinary work (Figure 1.2[14]) in recent years, and improvisation is central to this type of activity. Across the arts, sciences, and humanities these types of collaboration are viewed as important and an excellent way of developing innovative new work and making conceptual breakthroughs. Improvisation can be a crucial social and artistic process in helping to facilitate cross-disciplinary collaboration. Improvisation provides a method for collaborators to negotiate working together without being expert in each other's practice, skills, and knowledge. Improvisation is central in how this new

[14] https://vimeo.com/204860470

collaborative work is formed. One particular project we have introduced is *Concurrent*, an international network of researchers and improvisers who come together to share approaches and theoretical insights.[15] We also collaborate to develop new cross-disciplinary work with a particular interest in utilising psychological theory. In performances we consider how performers share or construct meanings while collaborating. *Concurrent* also focuses on testing emergent theory against diverse practitioner accounts of their practice with the aim of taking a holistic (theory and practice) view of collaborative cross-disciplinary practices.

Large ensemble improvisation

Another area of practice that has enjoyed an exponential growth in recent years is large ensemble improvisation. Large ensembles can incorporate all the features of improvisation discussed in the previous sections. They often include new technology, cross-disciplinary working, and they can also create new work in non-conventional performance spaces. Internationally, there are many large ensembles, often adopting the title "Improvisers Orchestra" (London Improvisers Orchestra,[16] Berlin Improvisers Orchestra,[17] St Petersburg Improvisers Orchestra[18] (Figure 1.3), Glasgow Improvisers Orchestra[19] (Fig. 1.4) The Royal Improvisers Orchestra[20]). These ensembles are a focal point for musicians from many different backgrounds (jazz, pop, folk, classical, electronic, etc.) to come together and create new work, new recordings, and new performances. They also attract artists from other disciplines

[15] http://www.concurrent.music.ed.ac.uk/
[16] http://www.londonimprovisersorchestra.co.uk
[17] https://berlinimprovisersorchestra.wordpress.com
[18] http://soundmuseumspb.ru/cd/1957-st-petersburg-improvisers-orchestra
[19] https://glasgowimprovisersorchestra.com
[20] http://www.yedogibson.com/page3.htm

Figure 1.3 Saint Petersburg Improvisers Orchestra. Photo credit: Saint Petersburg Improvisers Orchestra

to collaborate and explore innovative approaches to improvisation used in the development new work. There are unique challenges faced by musicians working in large improvising ensembles. In these groups responsibility for creative choices is distributed across a large number of people. Decisions about what to play and when to play and when to be silent and when to change what is being played are being made by performers on a moment to moment basis. Of course these types of issues and processes are at play within small improvising ensembles, but in large groups they become even more important since the sonic environment in a large improvising ensemble is significantly more complex. In a twenty-five-piece ensemble it is impossible for performers to be aware of every detail of what each person plays. Therefore, musicians need to be selective in their attention and sensitive in their decision making to find ways of interacting with specific co-performers. These types of unique creative challenges can facilitate new improvisational practices. Although improvisation will be the primary creative device, these ensembles may use elements of conventional notation or other compositional techniques within their practice. One example utilised by many large improvising ensembles is called conduction. This approach developed by Lawrence "Butch" Morris involves structuring musical material performed by large groups of

Figure 1.4 Glasgow Improvisers Orchestra collaborating with artist Cath Keay. Photo credit: Alex Woodward

players using hand signals (Morris, 2017).[21] A similar technique, Soundpainting, developed by Walter Thompson (Thompson, 2006) is often used in cross-disciplinary large group improvising incorporating dance.

Improvisation in education and well-being

The preceding discussion has focused largely upon improvisation within contemporary artistic practice; however, another vital feature of global Improvisational practice is its use in educational and health care settings. From an educational perspective, improvisation can be used to help children explore their creativity through music. In healthcare settings improvisation can facilitate

[21] http://www.conduction.us

psychological and social developments for participants who may not have any previous musical experience.

Play and informal group activities have long been recognised as a key part of children's social and psychological development (Rogoff, 2005). Improvisation is a crucial constituent part of children's play and interactions and is therefore fundamentally important in helping children establish lasting social bonds. Key features of these interactions are spontaneous unscripted improvisational moments. These moments of sophisticated decision-making are process-based rather than outcome-based, and the moment-to-moment interactions can be more important that any particular outcome objective. Less structured improvisational activities can facilitate new ideas as a key component of play and creative collaboration, helping children develop a sense of enjoyment and fun in social situations and facilitating creative breakthroughs. Educational activities involving improvisation can be used to develop new music skills not just with children but also with adults who have no experience of music making, or experienced musicians who lack confidence in improvising.

In music education, exercises with an improvised component can help children develop confidence in creative activities, as well as group skills and an awareness of collective music making (Stevens, Doyle, and Cooke, 2007). For example, a teacher stands in front of a class of twenty young children holding an outstretched hand with her palm facing the ceiling. When her finger touches her palm, she invites the whole class to sing in unison any note they wish. When she removes her finger from her palm, she asks the class to stop. She repeats this process five or six times and each time the class produce a rich textured chord. The children are exhilarated by the spontaneous generation of new music. They are also surprised at how conventionally beautiful this sounds. They are improvising since they simultaneously make their own choice of note resulting in an unforeseen impromptu chord. This exercise can be repeated on instruments to foster new technical skills in instrumental techniques; drums, pianos, guitars, or tuned percussion instruments can be used in to introduce children to new musical experiences. This approach has its roots in the conduction techniques of Butch Morris mentioned above (Morris, 2017). Some examples of the hand gestures are shown in Figure 1.5.

Community music, as a distinct field of practice, is a relativity new addition within music educational professional work (Veblen, 2007). It typically takes place outwith large institutional settings and emphasises non-hierarchical inclusive approaches to musical creativity (e.g., community percussion classes run out of a church hall or a community choir based in a room above a local bar). The pioneering work of drummer and educator John Stevens in this area of community music and improvisation has been particularly

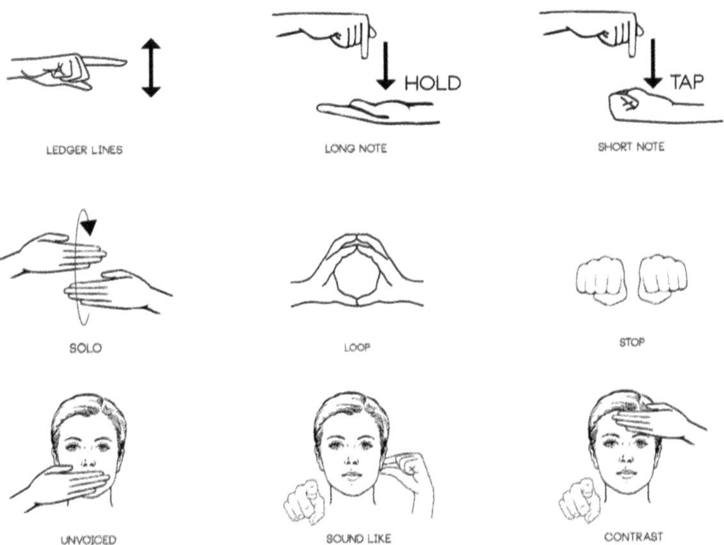

Figure 1.5 Examples of signs used in improvised conductions. Courtesy of Una MacGlone

influential over the past forty years. His text *Search and Reflect* (Stevens, Doyle, and Cooke, 2007), first published in 1983, contains a series of improvisational activities designed specifically to be used in community music settings. For example, in pieces called *Click and Sustain* participants are invited to sing a series of either very long notes (sustain) or very short notes (click) and explore the sonic environment by walking while singing. This is an improvisatory approach in that participants make choices about what notes to sing in the moments of execution, or about how loud to sing, or about timbral features of a note. This is an excellent exercise for introducing improvisation because although real time, in-the-moment choices are being made, the improvisational palette of choices is significantly reduced; being faced with limitless possibilities can sometimes be overwhelming for inexperienced improvisers.

Music therapists have traditionally operated in clinical settings that emphasise the developing relationship between client and therapist. Since music therapists work with individuals who may have problems communicating using conventional means, their practice is predicated on a sensitive and nuanced understanding of musical communication. To utilise music for therapeutic purposes, therapists must understand appropriate uses of improvisation in distinct settings such as a cancer ward in a hospital or schools for children with special educational needs. Improvisation allows for spontaneous, in-the-moment interaction to take place which can be profound and deeply emotional. The interactions may engage unconscious processes, and be creatively, cognitively, and socially engaging. These features can have significant positive effects on, for instance, problems arising from mood disorders or anxiety (MacDonald & Wilson, 2014; Stensæth, 2017). The health and wellbeing implications of improvisational processes are discussed in detail in chapter 7.

Improvisation as a contested term

The preceding discussion has outlined some of the key aspects of contemporary improvisational practice. However, the nature of improvisation can change depending upon the environment and circumstances. For example, a bebop saxophonist's improvisations will be quite different from a young baby's improvisations exploring a piano for the first time. This creates a dilemma for researchers endeavouring to make overarching inferences regarding improvisational activity.

For long periods of the twentieth century, improvisation was primarily seen as a defining feature of jazz music (Berliner, 1994). Jazz musicians' identities and livelihoods are developed and sustained on reputations for being an expert "improviser" (MacDonald & Wilson, 2006). Much of what we think about improvisation is shaped by performance practices in jazz and many researchers have provided detailed accounts and psychological theories of how jazz musicians generate and sustain ideas (Pressing, 2002). These tend to focus on the achievements of elite performers who have honed skills and craft over many years, understanding and assimilating the styles of the "jazz greats." While this approach to improvisation has been a crucial influence on culture worldwide and helped to make some of the most important musical breakthroughs of the twentieth century, these context specific accounts do not necessarily explain how improvisation functions in other music. This definition of improvisation may also inhibit people from attempting to improvise. Many experienced musicians (e.g., classically trained musicians), claim they cannot improvise. This may be because they have not learned to improvise within the jazz tradition and assume the stylistic features of jazz are expected to be present in all improvisation. It is also possible that conventional classical music education, in the broadest sense, may inhibit musicians from improvising due to the ubiquitous presence of notated music (Hill, 2017).

In addition to jazz and genre specific contexts for improvising, improvisation can also refer to a "post genre" or "non-idiomatic" form of music making. In many contemporary improvised music concerts, there are very few examples of overtly jazz, folk, pop, or classical stylings being performed by musicians who are as equally skilled as idiomatic improvisers. For example, Korean saxophonist Kang Tae Hwan and UK saxophonist John Butcher's performances and recordings are characterised by an almost forensic examination of the sonic possibilities of the instrument without recourse to the stylistic conventions of, say for example, jazz music or traditional Korean music. Venues such as Café Oto in London and The Stone in New York have become global hubs for experimental and improvised music and much of their programme focuses on what might be termed non-idiomatic free improvisation. The development of improvised music has reached a point where it is an idiom in its own right. There are many different subgenres and phrases used to describe improvised music: reductionist (free improvisation developed from minimalist approaches to music) and aleatory (chance events) are two. The same is true of approaches developed by some of the pioneers of free improvisation: Harmolodics (developed by Ornette Coleman) and Tri-axiom theory (developed by Anthony Braxton (J. Morris, 2012; Rush, 2017) are two examples. Non-idiomatic improvisation is usually taken to mean improvisation that has no stylistic conventions relating to a particular genre (e.g., a jazz swing feel or a folk music inflected rhythm). Thus, listeners and other musicians may not hear obvious references to a particular genre underpinning the improvisational gestures.

Many of the first generation of free improvisers came to free improvisation via specific genres of music, sometimes jazz but military bands and popular music were also influential in shaping these musicians' musical development (Toop, 2016). For example, in the UK, the roots of free improvised music are often discussed with reference to the pioneering work of saxophonist Joe Harriot in the late 1950s and then groups such as The Spontaneous Music Ensemble or AMM in the 1960s and The Feminist Improvising Group (FIG) in the 1970s (see Figure 3.1). Many of these musicians are still performing and in high demand (e.g., vocalist Maggie Nicols, pianist Irène Schweizer, drummer Eddie Prevost, or saxophonists Evan Parker and Trevor Watts).

Contemporary classical musicians may develop an interest in improvisation through an awareness of the notion of indeterminacy developed by Charles Ives and later Henry Cowell and John Cage (Ross, 2009; Toop, 2016). Indeterminacy emphasises chance events and spontaneous music making. For example, Cage's composition *Fontana Mix* contains the instruction "Intermittent gong attacks with crackles and screech" (Lochhead, 1994). By using this strategy, a piece can be radically different each time it is played, but still retain central elements and features that give the piece a character crucially linked to the composer. Indeterminacy has been treated as type of improvisation although John Cage was famously dismissive of improvisation (Toop, 2016). The term *indeterminacy* itself in some way favours the composer in that emphasis is placed upon the chance event—it is indeterminate—and not the performer. In this instance the performer is merely a conduit executing an instruction for the composer. The performer has less agency in this construction of spontaneous music making. Contrastingly, the term improvisation emphasises the agency of the performer as it is the performer who is making real time choices. *Indeterminacy* places agency, status, and power at the hands of the composer while *Improvisation* puts agency, status, and power in the hands of the performer.

While much of this book attempts to delineate specific features of improvisation it is important to point out that we are not suggesting a fixed definition. We propose some possible musical and psychological mechanisms with the aim of furthering our knowledge of what improvisation is and why it is important rather than as a way of clearly distinguishing it from other musical processes such as composition. Indeed, improvisation shares many features with composition and the popular idea of improvisation as "real-time composition" reflects this overlap.

The words "freedom" and "free" are often used to describe how improvising musicians work—free music, free improvisation, etc. These terms convey a sense of liberation, a lack of rules to be followed, or perhaps an escape from a more restrictive musical situation. However, when playing "free music" we choose what to play and when to play. These individual choices are always made in a relational context. Therefore "freedom," in music and indeed any context, is a relational concept. *Free from what?* and *free to do what?* are questions that follow from any discussion regarding freedom. For improvisers the notion of freedom and individualism is explicitly linked to collective responsibility. For example, musicians need to be sensitive to the overall sound world of the group when expressing individualistic urges. The desire for a saxophonist to express inner feelings via loud discordant tones may completely change a fragile lush texture developed by six string players within an ensemble. Therefore, in improvising ensembles, individualism and collective identity are constantly being negotiated through the ebb and flow of the collaborative endeavours of the performers. Freedom in music is quintessentially concerned with collective identity and responsibly since musicians play free in cooperative groups. Freedom is therefore more than "just another word for nothing left to lose," as suggested in Kris Kristofferson and Fred Foster's classic pop song "Me and Bobby McGee."

Overview of book

The preceding paragraphs highlight key features of contemporary approaches to improvisation. Improvisation has moved out of the shadows of artistic practice into a more mainstream position with festivals venues and promoters now presenting improvised events more than in previous years. New technologies facilitate new types of improvisational activity. Improvisation is now much more prevalent in educational contexts, and improvisation is also used as an artistic approach to foster collaboration between different cultural approaches to music making. These new frontiers of practice raise provocative questions for practitioners, researchers, and educators. For example, what is improvisation now and does all improvisation contain the same key elements? How do improvisers choose what and when to play when faced with infinite possibilities? How does an improviser in a group know what the others will do? Can improvisation improve our health and well-being? This book explores these questions in eight chapters each focusing on a different aspect of improvisation. Chapter 2 outlines different ways of conceptualising improvisation and why it is so important. It highlights different ways of thinking about improvisations and summarises previous theoretical accounts that describe the global processes involved. Chapter 3 explores the idea of improvisation as a universal capacity, providing evidence that everyone can improvise, not only musically but also as a primary human function; the ebb and flow of social life are propelled by improvisational interactions. Chapter 4 presents a new framework for describing and analysing improvisation and considers how improvisers decide what to play and when to play. It sheds a new light on improvisation, a process that that can operate at the pre-reflexive, preconscious level of awareness. Chapter 5 discusses shared understanding in improvising, emphasising that successful improvisation does not depend upon collaborating musicians having the same understanding of the meaning each musical episode. Chapter 6 argues that too much emphasis is placed upon traditional technical virtuosity when considering musical development and suggests new ways of conceptualising virtuosity in improvisation. Chapter 7 investigates the relationship between improvisation and health or well-being while chapter 8 points the way ahead and looks to future research and new developments in improvisational practice.

One aim of this book is to understand musical improvisation in its broadest possible context, and we will therefore present examples of musical improvisation from both inside and outside the jazz tradition. As stated at the opening of this chapter, this book is primarily about musical improvisation, but we will make links to other disciplines to highlight universal features of all improvisational activities. This is particularly important since one of the key features of improvisation is its capacity to facilitate cross-disciplinary collaboration.

To conclude, Derek Bailey (1993) famously wrote, in a quote that has adorned book chapters, articles, PhDs, and conference presentations ever since: "improvisation enjoys the curious distinction of being both the most widely practiced of musical activities and the least acknowledged and understood" (Bailey, 1993, ix).

This phrase, with the greatest respect to the author, is now redundant. Improvisation is now universally acknowledged and thriving in venues, festivals, and institutions around the world. While our understanding is developing rapidly, there is still much to be learned about how improvisations functions and this is a primary aim of this book. We aim to offer new insights on the psychological and musical processes and outcomes of improvisation by analysing how people talk about improvisation. Throughout this book we discuss what people say they are doing when they improvise with the aim of shedding new light on this universal, social, creative, and ambiguous process that is an elemental life force.

2
What's so special about improvisation?

Virtuoso improvisers sometimes have very little musical experience. Two eighteen-month-old identical twins stand facing each other in a kitchen. They have acquired no language in a conventional sense, yet they communicate with ooos and ahhs and paralinguistic melodic lines that demonstrate a sophisticated melodic and rhythmic awareness and a very nuanced understanding of turn taking.[1] By comparison, when Pandit Ravi Shankar and his daughter Anoushka Shankar performed in the UK as part of India and Pakistan's Golden Jubilee celebrations in 1997, the improvisations were intricate, technical, masterful, and steeped in centuries-old traditions of music making. The performance not only demonstrated a vast knowledge of improvisation techniques, but also complex cultural practices.[2]

Can we develop a theory that describes how improvisation works in these widely different scenarios? It may seem a tall order given the huge diversity of situations where improvisation occurs, however, in the following chapter we present different approaches to studying and theorising improvisation. The chapter reviews the ways in which improvisation has been understood by musicians and psychologists, setting out aspects of different theories and considering the assumptions that inform them. We propose some of key features of improvisation (it is creative, social, ambiguous,

[1] https://www.youtube.com/watch?v=lih0Z2IbIUQ.
[2] https://www.youtube.com/watch?v=9xB_X9BOAOU

The Art of Becoming. Raymond A. R. MacDonald and Graeme B. Wilson, Oxford University Press (2020).

DOI: 10.1093/oso/9780190840914.001.0001

and accessible) and outline different theoretical approaches (practice-based, cognitive, psychodynamic, neuroscience, and ethnomusicology).

Following a discussion of the various different theoretical approaches, we outline some gaps within these existing theories.

Defining improvisation

The aim to create an all-inclusive set of criteria that captures the richness of improvisation while retaining something unique about the process that distinguishes it from other activities, is ambitious. Does a newborn baby cooing and using her arm to coordinate her vocalisations with her father's lilting voice and gaze share basic features with Miles Davis's improvisations on *Kind of Blue*, one of the most famous and influential jazz recordings? If we define improvisation as any performance, with or without an intended audience, where some or all of what is performed is decided upon by the performers themselves in the course of that performance, then the answer is "yes."

Improvisation is creative

While defining creativity can be difficult, most definitions emphasise the act of creating something new using original ideas (Amabile, 1996). Using this broard definition, both these scenarios, Miles Davis and a newborn baby, involve creativity. Much has been written about the importance of Miles Davis's improvisations on *Kind of Blue*, and they clearly represent a good example of musical creativity. However, the musical improvisations and interactions of a newborn baby are perhaps less obviously creative. The urge to communicate, to reach out and connect emotionally and physically with others is a basic human capacity. This desire to communicate is not just an activity we want to do, but it is an activity we need to do. Communication is a biological and social imperative, and improvisation facilitates this need to communicate from birth. Improvisation manifests itself in unconscious and conscious musical gestures that are creative. Ground-breaking work has shown how parents communicate with newborn babies using creative and improvisational musical interactions that are fundamental to the human bonding process (Trevarthen, 2002). Creativity is unquestionably a difficult word to define but it remains a crucial activity studied, discussed, and researched (Hargreaves, MacDonald, and Miell, 2005). There is a strong predisposition to view creativity as an individual act and achievement but, as we point out below, creative acts are also collaborative acts.

Improvisation is social

The primary urge of the baby's communicative gesture in the father/baby example described previously is to connect with someone else and the responses unite two or more people in an improvisatory moment. Similarly, while a jazz musician's solo may draw attention to the individual musical features of the performer (melodic content, harmonic style instrumental technique, etc.) this all takes places within a group setting. The other performers, audience members, and listeners give the improvisation meaning and help shape its execution. For example, an unexpected chord played on the piano may influence a soloist to immediately play a particular note or phrase. The applause from a large audience can have a dramatically different effect on a soloist in comparison to the quiet nod of appreciation from an audience member in a sparsely populated small club setting. Therefore, all improvisation is social. Not only is the meaning of an improvisation shaped by the social context but the progress of the improvisation, the structure and the content is also influenced by the setting in which it is being performed. This

Figure 2.1 Improvisation workshop for children under age five at Glasgow Improvisers Orchestra Festival. Photo credit: Alex Woodward

is also true of the baby and parent interaction. Factors such as the presence of others and location will influence how parent and baby engage with each other. Thus, all improvisational interactions and their meaning are social and shaped by context.

Improvisation is universally accessible

We are all improvisers. The capacity to express ourselves and interact through music, to connect in an improvisatory way with others is available to everybody regardless of social, cultural, or educational background or any type of physical or mental illness. We are all musical and we are all improvisers. A newborn baby can connect with others though improvisation just as a virtuoso trumpet player can use improvisation to make deep emotional connections with an audience or other musicians. Figure 2.1 shows an improvisation workshop for children under five at Glasgow Improvisers Orchestra Festival. People engage in improvisation in a myriad of different ways. Also, there are many different types of aims and outcomes. A parent and a child improvising may have no explicit goals, but intimacy and connectivity are desired. A dancer improvising with a guitarist may be seeking to convey conceptual ideas related to specific movements and so the aims of these two improvisations are different. A key question for us is: "How can these be seen as the same process if the aims and outcomes are different?"

Improvisation is spontaneous

Interactions, musical, social, gestural, artistic, etc. often unfold in real time and those engaged in them are making moment to moment decisions about how those interactions will play out. Split-second decisions about what notes to play, what dance moves to make, when to leave a conversation, etc. occur in real time and are contingent on a myriad of constantly changing variables. Thus, improvisation is by definition spontaneous. Improvised work impresses and sometimes amazes us partly because we understand it to be created spontaneously, in the course of performance, unpremeditated.

Improvisation is ambiguous

Listeners interpret all improvisations, all music, all art through their own listening history and cultural experiences regardless of what particular emotion or meaning composers or performers wish to convey. Meanings are constructed by listeners and all music is therefore ambiguous. Musical meaning is in the ear of the beholder. This gives music a particularly strong resonance and is one of the main reasons why music is a powerful communicative medium. In most social activity we explain and discuss and negotiate what we are doing verbally; even in team sports, we can shout explicit instructions at each other. However, in improvised music this is not possible and so how can we take part in the same unpredictable musical event without explaining or cross-checking? This issue is discussed in detail in chapter 5.

In summary, improvisation is creative, social, accessible, ambiguous, and spontaneous. The combination of all these features makes it unique and ideally suited to utilising in a host of creative contexts to foster collaboration, new work, and conceptual breakthroughs. Going back to the previous examples at the beginning of the chapter (baby twins and Shankar duo), both duos are creating music that has never been heard before and will never be repeated. Each person's contribution is dependent upon what their respective partner is doing. Both examples involve sophisticated spontaneous collaboration. The meaning underlying the interactions is ambiguous because they are not explaining what they are doing as they go along. Also, both improvising duos use shared knowledge, shared social understandings, and a shared set of skills that make their improvisations unique.

Theories of improvisation

The preceding paragraphs offer a definition of improvisation showing it as a unique process. This next section summarises the way in which researchers have attempted to develop general principles that underpin improvisation. Each broad theoretical approach presented in the proceeding section foregrounds a different feature of the improvisational process. Practice-based theories emphasise the act of improvisation, while cognitive theories emphasise the mental processes that take place during improvising. Psychodynamic approaches foreground the ways in which unconscious processes can be expressed during improvisation, and neuroscience theories look to the anatomical brain structures stimulated during improvisation. The final approach presented in this section, ethnomusicological theories, place significant importance upon the cultural and social contexts within which the improvisation is taking place. These approaches are not presented as a comprehensive account of existing theories, but rather as examples of the broad range of possible ways to conceptualise improvisation practices.

Practice-based theories

There are a significant number of practice-based accounts of free improvising with many of the landmark texts written by pioneering musicians (Bailey, 1993; Oliveros, 2005; Nachmanovitch (2019); Prévost, 1995; Stevens, Doyle, and Cooke, 2007; Weiss, 2006). These practice-based accounts seek to highlight key aspects of improvisational practice and draw broad conclusions about the nature and importance of improvisation from the perspective of the writer who is also an improvising musician. Prevost (1995) links improvisational practice and in particular the musical choices made by performers to wider social and political issues. Bailey (1993) makes a distinction between idiomatic and non-idiomatic improvisation. Idiomatic improvisation is seen as improvisation that is rooted in a particular style or genre of music, e.g., jazz, flamenco, Indian Carnatic. This type of improvisation requires close adherence to rules (written and unwritten), conventions, and expectations. These guidelines include both explicitly musical (improvised melodies, harmonies, and rhythms) and also social features (when to play, when not to play, required deference, and on-stage, non-verbal interactions). By comparison non-idiomatic improvisation eschews these types of genre conventions by foregrounding improvisational processes as opposed to any particular style of music.

Cognitive theories

Cognitive approaches, such as those proposed by Berkowitz (2010), Pressing (1998), and Dean and Bailes (2016), emphasise internal mental activity undertaken by musicians when improvising. Borgo (2006) presents a unique multidisciplinary approach that draws on cognitive approaches to show the complexity involved in processes of improvisation. These accounts typically focus upon jazz musicians' cognitive processes and the neurological functioning that underpins improvisation. The sort of mental activities include: memory (scales, chords, phrases), learning (the mental processes underlying instrumental technique), perception (hearing chord changes, tonality, and harmonic intervals), attention (focusing on particular music elements, not being distracted, and coping with performance anxiety), conceptual development (broad-based structural approaches, bebop versus funk), and decision making. This approach to improvisation draws heavily on the metaphor of the brain as a complex computing system.

In one of the most influencial cognitive models Pressing (1988) presents a three-component information-processing model of improvising. This account involves sensory input, information processing, decision making, and motor output. The primarily physiological processes discussed include neurological and hormonal changes involved in improvising. Also described are the various fine grained and complex motor co-ordination tasks involved including how muscles, bones, and connective tissue execute the electrical instructions. Once the music is produced, sensory feedback mechanisms (auditory, visual, proprioceptive) create a constant and very rapid feedback loop. Another feature of Pressing's approach is a focus upon the development of musical ideas in terms of melodic, harmonic, and rhythmic phrases that are constructed, executed, and critiqued rapidly by the improviser as part of the feedback processes outlined previously. A key aspect is skill development and in particular the automatisation of motor and cognitive processing and execution. This takes place over time as the experienced improviser develops a vast repertoire of improvisatory skills, procedures, and gestures. Some of this automatisation is referred to as "muscle memory," a seemingly unconscious awareness of how to coordinate fingers, arms, toes, and legs when executing complex tasks (e.g., playing the piano, driving a car, playing tennis, etc.), and the whole central nervous and musculoskeletal systems are used in improvisation. There is some evidence to suggest that the notion of muscles having a "memory" is not just a metaphor. Recent neurological advances have pointed out that muscle memory may be produced by an ongoing thickening of the myelin sheaths around the axons of neurons. This ongoing myelination of axons is produced as a result of repetition of certain motor tasks. This myelination produces more efficient electrochemical conduction along neurons and this increased efficiently of conduction enhances "muscle memory" (Takeuchi et al., 2010).

Neuroscience approaches

A neuroscience perspective, while once again rooted in mental processes, focuses on the neuroanatomy involved in improvisation. One of the fundamental questions here is localisation of function. What particular parts of the brain are used in improvisation, and are they different from parts of the brain used on non-improvisational activities? Also, does using these parts of the brain while improvising confer any benefits over a long period of time? Rapid developments in brain imaging technology have facilitated significant gains in knowledge (Figure 2.2). One conclusion from this work is that substantially more regions of the brain are involved in music making than initially thought (Alluri et al., 2012). Donnay, Rankin, Lopez-Gonzalez, Jiradejvong, and Limb (2014) have highlighted idiosyncratic neurological features involved in improvising. Specifically, regions related to spoken language

Figure 2.2 Arja Kastinen improvising while wearing brain imaging technology in Curitiba, Brazil, in a collaborative project with Mari Tervaniemi. Photo credit: Elis Riberete

and syntax are activated while areas related to semantics (understanding spoken word) appear to be deactivated.

Psychodynamic theories

A psychodynamic approach to improvisation while still focusing upon underlying mental process looks more to the abstract and symbolic significance of improvisation. Psychodynamic theory holds that our personality, behaviour, and life choices are governed by a sensitive interplay between conscious and unconscious motivations. Unconscious desires and motivations manifest themselves in habits and day-to-day behaviours that we may be unaware of. For example, a need for punctuality may be related to an unconscious desire for control that dates back to very strict parenting. The nature of improvisation—with it being a spontaneous, real-time unfolding of musical ideas—therefore means it could be a prime site for the expression of unconscious motivations. A habitual desire to play loudly, for example, might be an expression of unresolved anger. This approach to improvisation has been extensively utilised within music therapy (see chapter 7).

Ethnomusicology theories

Ethnomusicological approaches have much to contribute to debates surrounding the importance of improvisation. As a discipline, ethnomusicology places an emphasis upon the cultural context, seeking to understanding musical engagement by incorporating wider social aspects. The methods and theories of cultural anthropology are particularly important. Nettl and Russell (2008) state that improvisation has played a minor role in musicological analyses of global music making. They cite Ernst Ferand's (1938) book, written in German, "Die Improvisation in der Musik" as being one of the first. However, these authors also highlight the ubiquitous presence of improvising across all musical cultures, giving detailed examples of improvising within Native American society, Iranian cultures, and a particularly striking account of how improvisation with Inuit cultures is used to help settle disputes. Here, people will sing their grievances to each other in public with improvised lyrics and melodies being part of the performance. The public are involved in helping to settle the dispute by assessing the quality of the contributions. Nettl and Russell (2008) discuss improvisation in non-Western non-jazz contexts and show a multitude of ways in which improvisational practices merge with social practices and operate as a key feature of social life. In Iranian musical traditions, for example, improvisation is highly valued as it signifies spontaneity and freedom. In Native American traditions the performance of improvised music can be accompanied and influenced by altered states of consciousness related to religious and social rituals (Nettl and Russell, 2008).

Nooshin (2003) outlines the importance of improvisation in both Iranian and Indian music, highlighting how performers do not reproduce a written score, and memorised material seems to account for a relatively small proportion of a complete performance of a råga or dastgah (types of traditional music). In these situations, the performer will extemporise upon a written guide and these extemporisations are clearly improvisational. There are similar accounts of improvisational practices given by Miller's (2013) analysis of Cuban flute playing.

Fischlin and Heble (2004) have produced a number of texts exploring the social and political significance of improvisation. While not coming from an exclusively ethnomusicological perspective, they focus specifically on the relationship between improvised musics, jazz and experimental music one the one hand and political discourse, political struggle and the politics of marginalised sections of society on the other. They explore how jazz and improvisation have been utilised to express highlighting, and challenge this marginalisation. Lewis (2002) discusses the political implications of improvisation, with particular emphasis on African American experiences. Importantly, he notes that renewed interest in improvisation in classical musical in the twentieth century in many cases neglected the contribution made by African American musicians and diminished the role of the improviser/performer while privileging the role of the composer. He summaries these ideas as Afrological and Eurological approaches to improvisation (Lewis, 2002).

Berliner (1994), in one of the most detailed and in-depth studies of jazz musicians' performance practices, highlights how musicians develop improvisatory skills and in particular provides intricate examples showing the type of focused musical work undertaken over many years that enables expert improvisers to perform. Monson (1996) focused upon the interplay between jazz players in rhythm sections via a series of interviews with leading players. She highlights the complex patterns of interaction involved in improvising and the key roles played by members of the rhythm section. This work emphasises the role played by other musicians in a band, not just the soloist, in developing improvisations. Borgo (2006) also focuses upon complexity in improvisation, innovatively combining ethnomusicology with cultural studies and cognitive science to investigate improvisation using chaos and complexity theory. He shows how improvisation can be understood as a complex system linking musical, philosophical, and cultural variables together. Born, Lewis, and Straw (2017) also present a multidisciplinary account that draws heavily on sociological and cultural theory focusing on the aesthetics of multidisciplinary improvising. Rose (2017) offers a phenomenological analysis of improvisation via interviews with practitioners and an examiation of his own practice.

These ethnomusicological approaches are important for many reasons, not least because they demonstrate the vast array of different cultural contexts within which improvisation takes place and they signal the inextricable link that exists between improvisation and wider social milieus. Ethnomusicology has helped demonstrate that understanding improvisation depends upon the social context.

In summary, these different approaches focus on different features of the improvisation process: the act of improvising or praxis (practice-based theories), mental process (cognitive theories), unconscious motivations (psychodynamic theories), neuroanatomy (neuroscience theories), and cultural and social issues (ethnomusicology). No one approach offers a comprehensive account of improvisation in its entirety, but each offer substantial insights into the processes and outcomes of improvisation across different contexts. However, a number of key issues need to be taken into consideration when assessing their utility and in the section that follows we move on to discuss some overarching questions to be addressed in the subsequent chapters.

Problems with existing theories

Output focused

Many of the previously discussed theories focus upon the outputs or musical products of improvisation while neglecting process-based elements and social contexts. For example, examining and analysing a transcription of a jazz solo can shed light on many important features of the improvisation, but it could also miss process and contextual features of how this solo was constructed. It may neglect the contributions of other musicians and the decisions that lead to the development of the improvisation. This is particularly relevant when we consider the tendency to canonise particular jazz standards and valorise the status of "the greats." It may also present a protectionist approach towards "expert" interests.

Contextually exclusive, genre-specific

The different approaches tend to be contextually exclusive and genre specific. For example, Johnson-Laird's work on how jazz musicians improvise may not translate to other types of improvisation (Johnson-Laird, 2002). A free improvisational approach may be less concerned with harmonic development based upon a set of predetermined chord changes and possibly more focused upon, for example, a slowly evolving sound scape where all the musicians are contributing long drone-like textures.

Focused on individual

Many theories of improvisation place the individual at the centre of the improvisatory experience, generating, selecting, and executing the ideas neurologically, cognitively, and physically. The reality of improvisation is that it functions almost exclusively in group contexts. Even individual solo performances by improvisers involve complex and reciprocal communication with audiences. This point is particularly important when we consider that many of the great jazz bands, whose influence reach far beyond the genre of jazz (those of John Coltrane, Thelonious Monk, Bill Evans, etc.), enjoyed stable membership over long periods. Bills Evans believed that building a musical and social rapport over a number of years with the same people was required for the type of work he wished to make (Petinger, 1998). Thelonious Monk and saxophonist Charlie Rouse worked together closely between 1959 and 1970 and their relationship was crucial in the development of Monk's music (Kelley, 2010). A shared social and musical history, developed over a long period of time, can be an important part of improvisatory relationships musicians develop together. This shared social history influences the ongoing improvisations and is a crucial psychological influence upon the music produced and how it is heard and critiqued. A comprehensive theory of improvisation must take into account these shared and influential social histories.

Viewing the individual as the primary point of study when analysing improvisation implicitly suggests that creativity resides within the individual. This approach often diminishes the importance of group factors and wider cultural variables, seeking to emphasise how some individuals have much higher levels of creativity than others. If improvisation is viewed as a social process that emerges in group situations, then social contexts become an important area of study. Research within the field of distributed creativity focuses upon these very features, investigating the nature of creativity when groups collaborate (Clark and Doffman, 2018). Improvisation is a fundamental aspect of distributed creativity. For example, a trumpet solo performed during a jazz quartet performance, for example, can be viewed as an emergent form of creativity, negotiated in the group, with all members involved in its development. Thus, the whole group is involved in producing the improvisation, which is unique to that group at that particular moment. Therefore, creativity is best understood as distributed across the whole group and not residing in just one musician. This distributed view of creativity challenges the "jazz greats" model of music history where the development of jazz is constructed via an understanding of the unique contribution made by individual players and composers across the twentieth century. Just as importantly it also challenges hegemonic views of creativity which tend to favour dead white men in art, science, literature, music, and indeed across all intellectual and creative endeavours.

One particular area where the focus is firmly on the individual is within neuropsychology. Due to the technological requirements of the procedures (MRI, PET, etc.), neuroimaging had, up until very recently, to focus upon the physiological functioning in one individual in order to gather data. Of course, this means that it can be difficult to research the neurological importance of the social context when the majority of studies are required to take place within a laboratory designed to gather data from one person. Several other limitations apply to neurological studies. For example, there is only room for one person in a scanner, participants lie horizontally, and some scanners are loud. This makes drawing inferences difficult since the experience of music in a laboratory scanner does not mirror real life experiences of music. New brain imaging technologies are emerging continually, and it is possible many of these problems will be overcome in the near future (Poikonen, Toiviainen, and Tervaniemi, 2018).

Some approaches not only acknowledge the importance of the group context but place primary significance upon how social processes can be a crucible for creativity. Mihaly Csikszentmihalyi's influential theories on *Flow* suggest emotional and cognitive fulfilment can be achieving by being in a state of *Flow*, where challenging but achievable goals are set and tasks are viewed as important and fulfilling (Csikszentmihalyi, 1991). Improvisation, as a social and creative process, is a key aspect of *Flow*. Social processes are paramount in Keith Sawyer's work, and he has published a number of texts foregrounding the importance of group processes in improvisation (Sawyer, 2012, 2013). His influential book *Group Genius* uses everyday examples like the invention of the ATM and the mountain bike to highlight the collaborative and distributed nature of creativity (Sawyer, 2008). Even in situations where one might assume decisive creative insights come from one person, he shows how these conceptual breakthroughs are group developments involving distributed creatively. Sawyer uses the term *group flow* to describe effective improvisation and collaboration. This approach can be used to describe group improvisation across different genres of music, different art forms, and in many social situations (business, educational, social, etc.). Important elements of achieving group flow include listening, focus, attention, equal participation, communication skills, and commitment to process (Sawyer, 2008).

Composer, performer, and improviser

Much of the published literature treats the distinction between composer, performer, and improviser as clear. However, the distinction is complex and in many instances a musician may be functioning in all three roles at once. During an extended improvisation, for example, a musician is clearly operating as a performer and improviser, but in the course of this improvisation the musician is also functioning as a composer as they are making decisions on a moment to moment basis about what notes to play, what rhythms to choose, what textures to explore, and what extended techniques to utilise. These decisions are all quintessentially composerly. Thus, an improviser is making composer-like decisions in real time and it is often said that improvisation is a form of real time composition. Comprehensive theories of improvisation must take into account the ambiguity of role and demarcation that exists between composer, performer, and improviser. One distinction between composition and improvisation is that conventional composition can be a private activity, away from the public gaze and may involve significant editing and revision before the results are placed in the public domain.

Treating improvisation as a separate form of activity from composing has implications about the type of discourse and the sort analysis that will accompany any critique of improvisational works. Often, composing is viewed as the most important type of creative musical endeavour and as a deeper, more serious, form of expression than improvisation, which by virtue of its spontaneity and real time execution can be construed as a more frivolous activity. The hegemony of Western music, built up over centuries, certainly places composition at the top of a clear and unambiguous hierarchy of musical creativity with the conductor on the next level of seniority and the performer below the conductor. The hierarchy continues for performers with the very clear power relationships within orchestras and soloists, first desk players, and rank and file musicians all have their relative statuses and perceived standing within the musical world. Improvisation allows us to blur the boundaries within musical hierarchies and to challenge existing hegemonies, power relations, and taken-for-granted statuses that exist within the musical and cultural world.

Assumptions of shared understanding

It is often said that a sign of a great improvising group is a shared understanding between performers regarding what is happening in the music on a moment to moment basis (Pras, Schober, and Spiro,

2017). However, shared understanding is not vital for successful improvisation and indeed even experienced improvisers who are performing in the same group will not share the same understanding of a particular moment in the music. What is important is that both or all the players are invested in the musical process and see meaning in that dialogue. It is the joint investment in the process that facilitates successful improvising. Very often in our studies two musicians will have different, but equally impassioned views of the same musical moment. As we and others have suggested, the meaning of all improvisations is ambiguous. Therefore, there is no objective truth in terms of what elements of an improvisation are good or bad or what improvisation decisions are correct or erroneous. Improvisers may have widely differing views on the meaning and quality of an improvisational moment. These views are all valid and may not in any way confound the quality of improvisation. The most important aspect of these group improvisations is that those involved are invested in the process and see an intrinsic worth in the moment-to-moment development of the improvisation. Thus, the socially constructed nature of meaning in group improvisation affords opportunities for group cohesion and a sense of collective purpose to emerge during these musical exchanges.

Summary

This chapter has proposed a definition of improvisation focusing on five unique components, namely, improvisation as accessible, social, creative, spontaneous, and ambiguous. It has presented practice-based, ethnographic, neurological, psychodynamic, and cognitive approaches to understanding improvisation and highlighted some problems with these existing theories and the assumptions that underlie them. These issues include the following: (1) A focus on the products of improvisation while neglecting process; (2) Existing accounts are genre specific; (3) A focus upon the individual while neglecting group processes; (4) Presuming clear demarcations in the roles and functions of the composer, performer, and improviser; (5) Assumptions of shared understanding between performers.

Experienced musicians can have serious concerns about their ability to improvise, or indeed perform music without a conventional score. This contrasts with the assertion and evidence presented in this chapter that improvisation is universally accessible. Therefore, there is a need to challenge current perceptions of improvisation, to get more people improvising, and to widen access to improvisational activities. Rather than improvising being viewed as an activity for elite musicians, it is important to democratise improvisation and make it not only accessible for everyone but also appreciated as an activity that is a vital part of children's early music education. We also need to consider the processes of construction taking place when people improvise together. In the following chapters we attempt to explain improvisation in a way that takes account of these issues bearing in mind that improvisation is social process. How does a social setting influence the music being produced? And how is that music discussed and how it is heard? In the next chapter we move on to discuss identities and highlight the importance of talking about improvising in how we hear and perform improvised music. Specifically, talking about improvisation crucially influences how we hear, and how we engage with improvised music.

3

Talking about improvisation

Constructing Identities

Music is always about more than music. The inextricable link music has to our culture, personalities, education, families, and friends gives it meaning and importance beyond sonic events or marks on a page. Music helps to define us, to shape our sense of self, and to construct our personalities. Furthermore, the language we use to discuss music is crucial to the musical and psychological processes involved in forming and maintaining identities (MacDonald, Miell, and Hargreaves, 2017).

In his wide-ranging lectures on music, pianist and conductor Daniel Barenboim has described improvisation as "the highest form of art" (MacDonald and Wilson, 2016). In doing so he acknowledges the skill, dedication, and virtuosity of musicians engaged in improvisation, situating improvisers at a particular peak of artistic prowess and aligning them with an elite group of musicians he had just been discussing in a public lecture. On the other hand, in the 2005 film *Charlie and the Chocolate Factory*, the character of Willy Wonka describes the improvised song of the Oompa Loompa workers as a "parlour trick" that "anyone can do," the kind of frivolous pastime that Bailey alludes to when he describes improvisation as a "doubtful expedient" or a "vulgar habit" (Bailey, 1993). When one of us (RM) described his improvised music to Scottish comedian Billy Connolly as "unlistenable music that nobody liked," Connolly replied that "if those jazz bastards don't like you, you must be doing something right." In this latter anecdote improvisation is

The Art of Becoming. Raymond A. R. MacDonald and Graeme B. Wilson, Oxford University Press (2020).

DOI: 10.1093/oso/9780190840914.001.0001

constructed as a practice around which strong expectations are held, for instance in relation to jazz, but one where oppositional approaches can bear fruit and develop positive new ideas. All these constructions of improvisation may be argued as valid but appear mutually exclusive.

This chapter highlights that we understand improvisation partly, or even largely, through talking about it. Talking about music is a fundamental part of how we make sense of music; through talk, we position ourselves as well as our views on music itself. This is especially so for professional musicians whose identities as musicians are central. Talking about music describes situations but does so through negotiation. Two musicians discussing a concert they have both just performed may exchange ideas on the good points and bad points of the music. They may reach an agreement, their views may differ, but the negotiated views exchanged will help construct how the event is remembered. Also, the version of the concert that emerges from this discussion can influence the music played in future concerts. In the three examples above, each speaker creates a separate version of improvisation. Rather than each version offering alternative and competing truths about what improvising is, each can be seen as constructing improvisation in a particular way that reflects the interests of those talking. Is improvisation really the highest form of art or just a parlour trick? In a single objective reality, it cannot be both. What this chapter argues instead is that definitions of improvisation emerging in talk serve specific psychological purposes for a speaker. When discussing improvising, speakers create, negotiate, and maintaining particular lines of arguments, and these lines of argument are linked to the musical identities and broader psychological identities of the speakers. Talking about improvising is important not just because it describes improvisation, but also because it constructs musical and social realities for those engaged in the dialogue.

This chapter makes the following key points:

- How improvisers talk about music shapes how they engage with music.
- Musical identities (defined later in this chapter) are important aspects of music making.
- Training improvisers to understand and articulate why they value the music they like should be an important part of improvisation pedagogy.
- Musical identities may be more important for improvisers than for other types of musician.

Talking about improvisers

In this section we develop our argument by analysing different types of talk about improvising. It is important to remember that we are interested in the psychological function of these descriptions. Here are four people saying something about improvising or what it takes to be an improviser.

Pedagogue Jamey Aebersold, in his bestselling text *A New Approach to Jazz Improvisation* (Vol. 1), emphasises that anyone can improvise. In seeking to demystify the process he sets out ingredients for a "good" jazz improviser:

> (1) Desire to improvise, (2) Listening to jazz via records, tapes and live performances, (3) A method of practice – what and how to practice! (4) A rhythm section to practice and improvise with . . . The old myth—"you either have it or you don't"—is strictly a myth which is founded on ignorance and the inability or unwillingness of those who can play to share, verbally, with those who think they can't . . . *Practicing exercises, patterns, licks, scales and chords should lead to more expressive creativity.* (Aebersold, 2012, p. 1)

Hindustani musician Wasanti Paranjape has this to say about improvising in the *khyal* tradition of Northern India:

> At first, it is very difficult to understand how to develop *alaps* in a *raga*. Students must listen to how other artists perform the same material, taking care to listen in an active manner. This way, they learn not only a *raga* and its *swara* (notes), but also perceive the full scope of skilful expressions, clever and sweet combinations of *swaras*, and different articulations possible in that particular *raga*. A pupil must also practice the *riyas* of a *raga* every day, learning notes, character, and mood—the *rasa* of the *raga*—and experimenting with different configurations and sounds. By imitating other artists and making small variations, she learns to create her own *alaps*. Improvisation is an intellectual and artistic process. It fosters a perception of music that can transcend the senses and the mind. The artist becomes submerged in the music, a state known as *rasanabhuti*. In the pursuit of artistic excellence, one effaces one's separate identity and gets absorbed into the experience of rasa. (Paranjape, 2012)

An article based on an interview with experimental musician Nikos Veliotis reports this:

> Although he has been frequently labelled an improviser and a cello virtuoso, he refutes both. ". . . Being an improviser is also a tag others use, but I don't think I've improvised at any point in my career. I always have a plan in my head and I tend to take my time in deciding. I don't think that has anything to do with improvisation." (Ignatidou, 2013)

From a dancer (O'Donnell):

> Improvisation has no destination decided in advance, and no obligations to any particular transmission of meaning. (Novack, 1990)

In an interview in *The Wire*, trumpeter Wadada Leo Smith stated that:

> I don't believe that musicians can be made. Don Cherry took a lot of amateurs and made great music from it. Background, maybe it's important in some contexts, but not always. (Freeman, 2010)

Comparing these different statements, one is struck by the differences in what is being implied about improvisation. Improvisation is variously described by these commentators as:

- *Completely explicable*—Aebersold talks of a "myth" that only certain people have what it takes to improvise.
- *Unfathomable*—Paranjape suggests that improvising "transcends the senses and the mind" and O'Donnell that it transcends "meaning."
- *Consciously intellectual*—an artistic process involving experimentation and the application of learned material (Paranjape again).
- *Instinctual*—Paniotis implies that planned or decided music is something other than the reactiveness of improvising.
- A *specialist* vocation—Aebersold and Paranjape both stress the extensive knowledge and skills that an improviser should acquire thorough study and practice, and the dedication or motivation required to persevere through the considerable effort involved.
- Something that can be great if played by *amateurs*—Smith argues that rewarding improvised music can be made by people without background experience.

- A practice that builds on *tradition*—the ability to execute particular licks or alaps is held to be essential to improvising in jazz or khyal.
- A practice that has *no relation* to existing meanings—O'Donnell asserts that his practice bears no responsibility to existing traditions.

How can improvisation be explicable yet unfathomable, intellectual yet instinctual, specialist yet amateur, traditional yet unfettered by expectations? From this usage it seems that improvisation might be too elastic a term to have much practical use in defining an activity consistent with a huge range of behaviour. The suggestion that broad definitions of improvisation become too generic to have any intellectual and practical traction when trying to develop new insights may seem logical. However, these statements from individuals diversely involved in creative industries underline that improvisation is an artistic practice that practitioners are frequently called on to explain or define (or indeed distance themselves from). Opportunities and livelihoods may depend on how this is done. While we might romantically believe that music, dance, or art speak for themselves and that, for instance, music of quality will inevitably be recognised as such, most of those involved in the performance or promotion of improvised arts inevitably find that attracting audiences, financial support, or recognition, or communicating their approach to students or interviewers requires them to make a case for what they do. We are thus surrounded by accounts of improvisation; considering the source and circumstances of those definitions can go a considerable way to explaining why they may appear drastically different.

We have pointed out how accounts of free improvisation in the media differ in key aspects from accounts that are offered in the course of research and understood to be confidential (Wilson and MacDonald, 2017). We have also found differences in the ways that musicians from different backgrounds talk about improvising

(Wilson and MacDonald, 2012). Some of the same can be seen in the quoted material in the previous section. All those ways of describing improvisation are tenable theories to explain how it is achieved, each consistent with particular beliefs.

Aebersold's words are presented to preface what has become one of the world's most successful teach-yourself publications on jazz. In refuting that improvisation might only be achievable by a select few gifted individuals, he is addressing an imagined audience of potential customers wanting to be able to play improvised solos along with a jazz rhythm section, but lacking knowledge and experience. Paranjape is addressing the readership of an academic journal published in a Western country as a representative of a musical heritage in a non-Western country asserting the same prestige as Western musical canons. Her words are informed by particular assumptions, for instance, that the music is exotic and unfathomable (terms are given in Hindi then explained, and it is stressed that the music is hard to understand), or that an improviser is someone in pursuit of artistic excellence. The writer reporting on the interview with Veliotis positions "improviser" as a "label" to be resisted. He implies this would be an incorrect interpretation of what Veliotis does, one that does not reflect the more privileged understanding of this music that he and Veliotis share. Veliotis, addressing a presumed readership of aficionados of arcane and ground-breaking music, seeks to distance himself from what he refers to as a "tag," an uninvited pigeonholing. He positions improvisation as something less considered or deliberate than what he does. Smith is addressing an interviewer for a specialist music magazine (*The Wire*) and aligns himself with particular figures likely to be known to and appreciated by that readership: trumpeter Don Cherry's music is invoked as an example that is likely to be known, or should be known, to the interviewer and their readers.

In the language of the social sciences, these different versions of improvisation can be understood as shaping particular *identities* for the speakers—as professionals, as "outsiders," as trendsetters, or as free spirits. We argue in line with mainstream psychological theory that the concept of identities must be taken into account when considering how any individual speaks about improvisation, since their talk will be informed by particular *musical* identities.

Musical identities: negotiated in talk

We all have musical identities. As our lives have become more unpredictable and increased choices open up for us in terms of employment, travel, relationships, gender, etc. and how we want to spend our lives, identity has become a key concern for modern life (Giddens, 2001). When we express the various ways we may consider ourselves to be musical: "I only sing in the bath," "I am an opera singer," "I play a few Bob Dylan songs," these statements are identifying us as musical in particular ways. These types of statements about our musicality are important markers of musical identity. Our musical tastes also act as a cultural signifier of identity and this musical identity feeds into, and is influenced by, our general sense of identity. It is in our talk that we construct and negotiate these identities. Talking about music therefore influences music listening but also music making. Identity as a musician is worked up by claims of what "you" would do in this identity. In these accounts discourse not only functions to fulfil identity needs for those talking but also helps to shape their experiences of playing music. This distinction between using music as a resource in general identity work (a person may discuss their love of concerts where they can mingle with friends) and using music in the development of identities that are specifically musical (I am a singer in a community choir) is defined in terms of "Identities in Music" and "Music in Identities" by MacDonald, Hargreaves, and Miell (2017). They arise in particular contexts (e.g., a conversation between band members, or an interview for a music website) and are therefore multiple for any one individual; one's identity as a musician depends on whom one is talking to. Additionally, musical identities are multifaceted in the sense that our musical identities are composed of different features. For example, a professional musician's musical identities include elements such as musical tastes, education, family environment, friendship groups, etc. All these features will be influential when considering how musicians improvise and the choices that are made during these improvisations.

If talking about improvisation is an important part of the improvisation process, or influences how we engage with it, one obvious approach for researching this field is to ask improvisers what, why, and how they do what they do. Their answers could be read as an "authentic" description of events, thoughts, feelings, or experiences. However, the social constructionist model of communication views language use as type of social action. People are seen as being able to achieve certain personal and social ends through their talk (Potter and Edwards, 1992; Potter and Wetherell, 1987), rather than using it purely as a means of transmitting information. The responses musicians give in interviews function not only to describe events but also to construct or reconstruct them (Puchta and Potter, 2002). In responding to questions about their musical lives, musicians are presenting particular versions of themselves and the events they are involved in. This may be thought of as an identity *project*. For example, when discussing musical preferences, they are not just conveying tastes for a musician, band, or piece of music, but they are also engaged in important personal "business" or identity work by positioning themselves (for example, as aficionados or experts) in relation to others. Jazz is presented as collaborative practice utilising popular "psychological" constructs, such as Czikszentmihalyi's "flow" (MacDonald and Wilson, 2006). However, these accounts function to create, maintain, and negotiate identities, rather than reflect any objective "truth." In many respects jazz is whatever jazz musicians say it is at the time. This is not to suggest that musicians are liars, but rather to highlight that when musicians are asked questions about their practices the answers given are not simply descriptions of events, thoughts, or feelings; rather, they *become* the events, thoughts, and feelings. Thus, in our analysis we can move beyond a simple truth and reality model to investigate the psychological function of the language used in interview scenarios.

Jazz identities

We adopted this social constructionist position in a series of interviews with UK-based musicians to develop new understandings about how the participants viewed their musical lives, identities, and in particular their improvising. Speaking to focus groups (MacDonald and Wilson, 2005) we found that musicians did agree on features that could loosely be termed "the jazz life," a demanding lifestyle created by an eclectic professional practice. These corresponded broadly to the following: struggling with competing priorities as a professional musician, struggling to be understood by audiences and institutions, and not being paid properly. However, while categories such as "maintaining swing feel" and "a balance of collective and individual practices" were proposed as important, musicians struggled to agree on the defining features of jazz music. As one participant put it[1]:

> *if you asked other jazz musicians they would say something different, they might. I'm just saying certain musicians.) See, they prioritise different things in the music for themselves. I would agree the swing thing kind of is a defining element but that's me and whoever's here. You know. There are certain musicians that we widnae work wae. Who've got probably different ideas. I mean*

[1] We have used spelling conventions for spoken Scots to give a faithful rendition of what interviewees actually said.

everybody's got a different idea of what jazz is(.) anyway I'll get ma coat.

We also identified particular and distinct types of talk in the interviews and termed these styles "mastery" and "mystery" repertoires. In the mastery repertoire, improvisation was viewed as an activity that required advanced technique and considerable input of time and energy over an extended period of time in order to achieve the ability to improvise. Negotiations involve handling discrete repertoires of mastery and mystery in accounting for improvising (Wilson and MacDonald, 2005).
For instance, another participant stated:

> *Yeah it doesn't magically happen. There has to be effort and there has to be some degree of training. It doesn't necessarily have to be formal but you have to be listened and researched and I don't think, a lot of people don't realise the amount of effort that goes into it.*
>
> *The experience is not just "do it" or "you can't do it" you know. Yeah I don't think improvisation is something that you've either got or not got. I think it's a skill that you can learn just the same as any other skill.*

These two extracts emphasise a belief that any individual who wishes to improvise needs to spend time developing specific skills. This time can be spent listening or practicing, in formal or informal situations. The mastery repertoire thus focuses upon skill development as a necessity for improvisation.

The mystery repertoire, on the other hand, emphasises the ineffable, soulful, or esoteric features of improvisation, its instinctual uncontrolled and qualities. In the examples that follow, the less technical aspects of improvising are foregrounded.

> *Which is another point about improvising, when you're truly improvising you're playing with this intensity. And y-you don't really*

> *care what, mistakes just go by and (mmhm) it's like, doesnae matter cause you're playing with intensity and (.) and passion // and*

This quote emerged in the same interview, from the same speaker, as one of those above illustrating the mastery repertoire. In other words, he adopted different accounts of improvising depending on the conversational context. Treating these repertoires as flexible rhetorical devices and not as statements of fact invites consideration of what they do for musicians' identities. For example, adopting the mastery repertoire attaches acquired value to being an improviser; therefore, musicians employing it can construct a set of criteria around improvising that emphasises their achievement, and therefore capital, social, cultural, or otherwise. However, we have argued in the previous chapter that the same mechanism of spontaneous experimentation is involved in improvisation across a wide spectrum of objectives and abilities: hugely different music may be generated, but it all comes about in essentially the same way.

These findings emphasise that beliefs about what is required to improvise *are* beliefs (constructed in talk, rather than reported facts) and demonstrates negotiation and fluidity of ideas about improvisation. It might be wondered whether talk about improvising is more a concern for social science, rather than the purely musical concerns of music. Yet these patterns of discourse have a vital role in shaping our relationships to music making, in how we go about it, and how we are able to access this area of life.

Hegemonic identities

When researching the discourse of jazz we suggest that it is important to move beyond the reporting of talk as a simply a reflection of truth or objective reality, and to take into account issues such as *hegemonic identities.* We use the term *hegemony* to mean a set of cultural norms that preserve the status of powerful group.

Language is inevitably used to favour dominant cultural positions, whether consciously or unconsciously (Wetherell and Edley, 1999). Hegemonic power relations are manifest in ideas, perceived norms, or expectations that are taken for granted as truths, and serve to reinforce the positions of the most powerful people within a diverse cultural milieu. Importantly, hegemonic identities are manifest in many situations where speakers may not be conscious of these issues, e.g., a middle-aged male discussing gender issues in politics may not be aware of the hegemonic power structures that have culminated in relatively few women making a career in politics. Such hegemonic influences are apparent in the identity work of musicians describing their practice. Figure 3.1 shows The Feminist Improvising Group FIG who were explicit in challenging hegemonic masculinities in their performances during the 1970s and onwards. In our (all-male) focus groups we found musicians' talk reflecting masculine hegemonic identities (Wetherell and

Figure 3.1 Feminist Improvising Group (FIG). Left to right: Corinne Liensol, Maggie Nicols, Georgie Born, Lindsay Cooper, Cathy Williams

Edley, 1999). Since jazz and improvised music is dominated by male musicians and masculine identities, the way in which some musicians discuss their practice served to reinforce the dominant positions of masculine identities within the music. This can be seen in the two quotes that follow.

> *that's the quality of a good soloist in all styles, you know, people are there, and they have to have the balls to say "you're gonna listen to me now," you know.*
>
> *all you are thinking about is the 30 quid at the end of the gig and that lassie's tits*

Whether or not the language used here was a conscious attempt by male musicians to exclude female musicians from playing jazz cannot be determined, but the discourse is less concerned with a biologically gendered identity than with maintaining a socially constructed account of gendered actions. Metaphorically, woman can still have the "balls" to play improvised music, but the use of this particular metaphor serves to legitimise and prioritise a masculine identity, if not biology, in the performance and experience of improvising. The objectification of a female audience member in the second quote is rendered as humorous, allowing the speaker to maintain an ironic distance, but still serves to normalise a stereotypically masculine identity within the discourse of jazz musicians.

We subsequently undertook a series of interviews with both male and female improvising musicians (MacDonald and Wilson, 2006). In these interviews, the female interviewees tended to prioritise skill as a performer over the negative consequences of gender stereotyping from colleagues or the general public. While negative experiences arising from sexist talk were reported, their accounts asserted that skill, dedication, and professionalism meant that they were not held back because they were highly skilled performers. In some senses the musicians are proposing a meritocratic system where, regardless of the social structures in place, quality and excellence will triumph. This type of language is discussed by Gilbert and Mulkay (1984) who term it a "truth will out" device. In their work scientists accounted for the acceptance of their own work as being entirely related to quality—if the work is good eventually it will be accepted. Following Gilbert and Mulkay, we termed this type of language among our jazz interviewees an "experience will out" device (MacDonald and Wilson, 2006). We observed that meritocratic jazz identity is preferred in opposition to a gender identity which recognises that sexism may hold female jazz musicians back but implies an appeal for special consideration, undercutting claims of objective merit. This work has relevance for initiatives on a global level aimed at increasing opportunities for female musicians and composers across the whole musical spectrum.

Hegemonic power relations also influence how individuals feel about improvising in general. Many people are put off improvising because they assume they do not know what they are supposed to do, or lack understanding of music. Some psychological and practitioner theories reinforce this, suggesting prerequisites such as familiarity with definitive works or the acquisition of facility and expertise in musical skills such as chord recognition or executing complex rhythms. Contrastingly, infants, with no specific genre knowledge, improvise musical interactions effectively and beautifully with their parents and each other. The centrality of improvisation to music therapy, where clients need no prior musical knowledge, underscores that improvisation is a fundamental process that can be engaged in at any level and is aligned with other human behaviours. If approached in this way, improvisation offers a vital way into creative engagement with music, and people can feel ownership of the music they make without concerning themselves about whether they are doing it "right." Research evidence discussed previously presented the views of jazz improvisers and of free improvisers to demonstrate that ideas of prerequisite knowledge or abilities are strongly subjective, and often reflect identities associated with professional practice. These issues are arguably more important for improvisers than for other types of musician. To develop as an improviser explicitly requires regular social and musical interaction with others, since a large part of the creativity emerges in the moment of a group paying.

Hegemonic identities reflect power structures analysed by other researchers; for instance, Lewis (2002) has highlighted the "Euorological" assumptions underpinning some authors' account of the development of improvised practices in Western art music (Figure 3.2). The discourse attached to Eurological approaches to improvising prioritise the role of the composer within improvised music whereas Afrological accounts place more importance upon the spontaneous translation of emotions and thoughts into music of the performer.

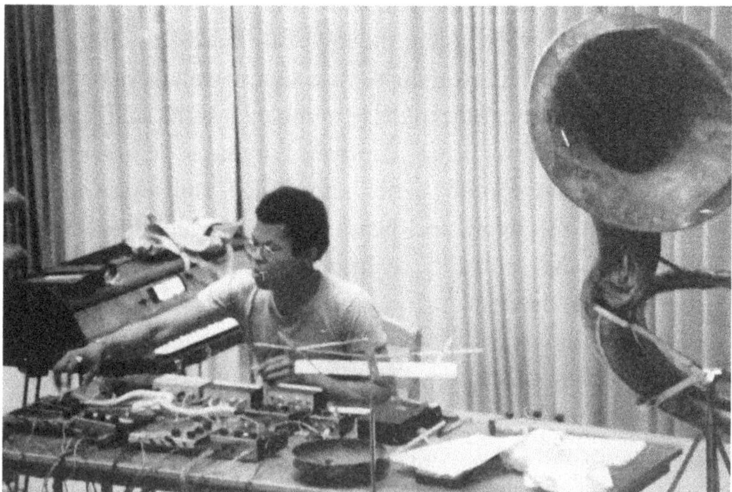

Figure 3.2 Improviser, composer, and theorist George Lewis, pictured in 1975. Photo credit: Nancy Carter

Summary

Beliefs about what is required in order to improvise are constructed in talk. We have highlighted in this chapter the negotiation and fluidity of these beliefs. Many people feel unmusical or unable to improvise because they feel they lack the required skills or knowledge. However, assertions that these are necessary are being generalised from what is necessary to maintain particular identities. Mastery repertoires overlook improvisation that takes place in informal settings. For example, children's first musical experiences are by definition improvisatory. Exploring a piano for the first time perhaps pressing the keys or banging the side of the piano can be sonic adventure for children—a quest for new sensory experiences. Children may not be concerned with notions of right and wrong notes but rather adopt a playful investigation of the instrument. The mystery repertoire affords the possibility of naïve improvisation, but positions the improviser as a channel for creativity rather than possessing the potential to reflect on and choose what they play. In Paranjape's words quoted earlier, "one effaces one's separate identity and gets absorbed into the experience." Asserting that improvisation is universally accessible, on the other hand, is consistent with a belief in universal and conscious creative engagement that *can* fashion separate identity.

We need to attend more carefully and deliberately to how improvisation is talked about in classrooms and community music settings to prevent people being put off trying to improvise. In terms of Pressing's three-stage cognitive model of improvisation discussed in the previous chapter, it could be argued that while there is extensive provision for education in the executive aspects of improvising (developing knowledge), the generative (ideas) and evaluative (deciding whether the improvisation is any good) components have little or no pedagogic practice to support them. Extensive works and methods exist to help aspiring musical improvisers acquire facility with widening the range of what they can play instantaneously. These texts are aimed to help musicians to apply these techniques within harmonic or rhythmic structures and how to play and assimilate what previous famous improvisers have recorded. Relatively little exists to suggest how a novice improviser might work to develop or change the way they generate musical ideas through improvisation. In the frame of reference of the mystery repertoire, it is as if, having consciously amassed skill and knowledge to a sufficient degree, inspiration is then expected to arrive through some subconscious process to turn these skills into music. The often-quoted aphorism "You have to learn the rule book and then throw the book out of the window," used when discussing how to learn to play jazz, is a good example of this notion. An emphasis on canons of previous greats also tends not to foster critical evaluation when developing as an improviser. Many texts on improvising end with lists of recommended listening, to be diligently assimilated. Yet if one is to evaluate emerging musical ideas as part of an intense real-time process, a confident and nuanced awareness of personal musical value would seem to be valuable. Training improvisers to think about what they themselves want to play and why, and to understand why they value the music they like, should be a large part of improvisation pedagogy. How we talk about music becomes absolutely fundamental within this approach. In training individuals to improvise, it should be considered important that learners are encouraged to reflect on what they and others are doing, and that learners are supported to express this the way they see it. Being able to articulate one's practice to others can be seen to be a vital part of making one's way as an improviser; indeed, the way one can describe it may shape the way one behaves as an improviser with others.

Research implications

The arguments made in this chapter have important implications for research. If we cannot assume improvisers to be giving an objective factual account of what they have experienced when they talk about improvising, how can psychologists or ethnomusicologists expect to cast light on how this takes place? This is close to the "black box" paradigm of behaviourist psychology: improvisation as an internal, inaccessible process that can only be understood through analysis of its output, improvised music, or, perhaps, via the newly emerging field of neuroimaging of improvisers in action.

We would argue against this view. Firstly, important insights have emerged from studying what improvisers say about improvisation. For instance, the understanding that improvisation within time-based or metrical forms may take place through a process of "chunking" previously acquired materials (e.g., Norgaard, 2011) has replaced the more romantic vision of melodies springing fully formed into the imagination of an improviser as they play. This has most convincingly been argued by researchers asking improvisers to describe what they were doing when they improvise. However, the very fact that inconsistencies and subjective influences are apparent when improvisers talk about what they do points to the more important understanding that what improvisers do is almost certainly influenced by how they and others talk about it. Even if improvisation is verbally inaccessible at the point of execution, this does not mean that we can regard it as a unitary, objective behaviour that is somehow variously misrepresented when people try to describe it. Rather the myriad ways that people come up with spontaneous music or dance when they are with other performers is better explained by the idea that the infinite complexity of social interaction and social construction has a primary shaping hand in what they do.

In music, a closer interaction between qualitative social researchers and musicologists is likely to enhance our understanding of improvisation considerably. Whereas in the past these fields of enquiry pursued relatively separate paths (musicologists tend not to cite psychological research, and music psychologists tend only to mention musicological findings briefly as part of an introduction or conclusion), a strong dialogue and exchange of analyses on how an improvisation can be understood as an organisation of sounds and as an organisation of people, and how these two views intersect, has the potential to offer new insights into the black box.

The same can be said for collaboration between researchers into improvisation in different disciplines. While qualitative researchers in music dance and performance art may seek to capture what goes on by talking to improvisers in their own disciplines, those researchers rarely if ever see whether improvisers in another discipline talk about what they do in the same way. The social interactions between dancers improvising might be expected to be different from those among musicians, given the higher level of embodiment associated with the discipline and the stronger emphasis on visual processes (compared with musicians, dancers and visual artists are a lot less likely to improvise with their eyes closed). Bringing these separate streams of qualitative enquiry together should be enormously fruitful for our understanding of talk and improvisation. In the following chapter we focus on this conundrum by proposing a model of improvisation that attempts to describe all forms of cross art form improvising.

4
Stones, Clouds
A new model for improvising

A minute is a long time in music. Within it we might expect to find evidence of whatever creativity characterises the piece or its performers. Taking a minute from each of three musical improvisations raises questions about the role of the individual in relation to the group.

The Australian ensemble *The Necks* are celebrated for their spontaneous music making, describing their own live shows as "sustained improvisations." During a minute from one of their live performances,[1] Chris Abrahams on piano switches from outlining a reverberating arpeggio to sounding slow octave trills on a series of descending notes. Bass player Lloyd Swanton briefly bows long notes following the pianist's octaves, while the drummer Tony Buck begins to sustain a wash of sound on one cymbal.

During the first minute from a live performance by Geri Allen, Esperanza Spaulding, and Terry Lynne Carrington of Allen's piece "Unconditional Love," the pianist repeats a short group of notes over two chords, punctuated twice by a cluster of notes higher up the piano.[2] Spaulding plays a melodic line of plucked notes on bass that match the tonality and rhythm of the piano, but are constantly varying in rhythm and pitch while returning at regular intervals to the tonic of Allen's first chord. Drummer Carrington enters after a short interval and plays semiquavers on her hi-hat in time with the

[1] www.youtube.com/watch?v=DFpWd1V__SI, 1:54 to 2:45.
[2] www.youtube.com/watch?v=XHs-pNjC4eo

The Art of Becoming. Raymond A. R. MacDonald and Graeme B. Wilson, Oxford University Press (2020).

DOI: 10.1093/oso/9780190840914.001.0001

others, punctuating this as she goes on with varied patterns on the snare rim and bass drum that synchronise with Spaulding's melody.

In another minute from saxophonist Evan Parker's solo improvisation "Aerobatic 4" (Parker, 2009, track 4, 2:00 to 3:00), we hear him move from stuttering rapid runs of semi-stifled notes across the extended range of the soprano saxophone. He intersperses these with an array of sustained notes, hums, and growls, then proceeds to short bursts of rapid-fire articulation on an expanding range of notes that gradually becomes louder, more frantic, and underpinned with growling. Suddenly he bursts into long muted notes that outline a melody in the harmonic series, with outbreaks of flutter tonguing.

We have defined improvisation as a performance where the performers make choices about what to play. Yet certain features of these examples of improvised music are notable:

- a large proportion of what is played consists of repeated or sustained material
- within the ensembles, individual players vary what they play at different rates, or to different extents
- some choices seem determined by what another group member is doing (e.g., what Swanton and Carrington play), while others are not obviously informed by anyone else (as with Parker and Buck).

Are all three examples creative or improvisatory in the same way?

This chapter will consider what psychologists mean by creativity, and argue that the choices of the players in the preceding examples share the same basis even if they result in very different musical outcomes. We will consider evidence from interviews with improvisers to offer a novel understanding of how group improvisation in all manifestations follows a common creative process, with the negotiation of decisions at its heart—a process which can lead to creative outcomes that are not foreseen by anyone involved.

Creativity and the individual improviser

A piece of music can surprise or intrigue us when we hear it for the first time, or it may manipulate or amplify an emotional state in ways that cause it to remain with us for years. These qualities are likely to make us attribute creativity to whoever came up with this music. Creative acts are defined in psychology as those that possess *both* novelty and value for either an individual, a group or a society (Amabile, 1996; Sawyer, 2012). Traffic sounds or the movements of commuters in a train station emerge in novel configurations every day without us noticing or valuing them, so are not typically seen as creative. Tribute acts are valued for their ability to replicate familiar pop classics without novelty, and so are not praised for their own creativity but for their veracity. Creativity at a social level (or "big-C" creativity) is understood to be a scarcer phenomenon than that at an individual level, since it is easier to come up with something that surprises and intrigues one person than something unfamiliar and rewarding to a whole society. As a result, the degree to which artistic outputs are innovative in cultural terms reflects their perceived value; thus, the world of fine art has been held up as a social realm where uniqueness and consistent innovation at a cultural level are idealised (Becker, 1984).

The creativity of improvisation can be understood in these terms. While aleatory or indeterminate music is understood to be generated by random processes beyond the performer's control (Beil and Kraut, 2012), most improvised music is valued on the assumption that exciting *new* sounds are being deliberately shaped in performance by individuals choosing to do so in ways they have not done before. Making such artistic choices is an activity that creates considerable cognitive demands, even when it is not undertaken in real time. It has been influentially argued that a musician can only cope with inventing a continuous rapid melody on a minute-by-minute basis if they limit their choices to familiar options, and if they have learned to constrain what they play within pre-existing styles or "referent materials" (Pressing, 1987). This accounts for the emergence and reproduction of *genres* of improvised music. Audiences for Indian classical music, for instance, recognise the improvised melody of a *raga* as an accomplishment because prescribed patterns of notes are deployed within time-honoured structures, albeit in novel combinations that are chosen during performance.

However, such theory does not account for paradigmatic innovation in improvised music: those improvisations that break the boundaries of what is recognisable. When Ella Fitzgerald, on her famous 1945 recording of "Flying Home," began improvising non-verbal vocal lines, the rhythms and chord extensions she used went far beyond whatever conventions existed at the time for "scat" singing (Nicholson, 2004). Yet what she sang, new to the world of jazz and abandoning its stylistic constraints at that point, continued to be accompanied by her band and appreciated by critics and audiences. The improvisers involved in episodes such as these are somehow able to reach beyond what they knew to execute and accommodate music unheard of at the time, transforming generic music into something unrecognisable even to some of its former practitioners. The fact that such moments are among the most valued achievements in jazz shows improvised music functioning as "art music" in Becker's terms (Becker, 1984). In fact, the ethos of the "non-idiomatic" free improvisation that crystallised in the 1990s attaches value specifically to music sounding like nothing that has gone before (Bailey, 1993).

In improvisation as in other human endeavours, creativity is assigned to choices that result in innovative and valuable work. Existing psychological theories explain how improvisation can be creative at an individual level within a genre but do not explain the more rarefied level of social or cultural innovation where existing genre practices are transcended. This may reflect a tendency to view creativity as being exercised by individuals (Sawyer, 2006). If an individual feels that deciding what happens in a piece of music is up to them, they can base this on what they already know and like, and know they can do. A solo improviser is master of what they play; anything created is produced by them in isolation, and they will only create what they alone can imagine. Yet when a group improvises, there is a perpetual level of uncertainty for the individual over what the others may choose to do, and what effect their own playing might have on the group.

If this sounds like a recipe for chaos, the next section considers how we might explain the creation of music that no one person is in control of.

Creativity in group improvisation

Creativity underlies both the commodification of musical recordings or performances and the teaching of music, in that individuals seen as highly creative are treated as having something rare and valuable to impart to their fans or students. It is perhaps most easy to commodify as a characteristic of one person. Mainstream jazz works are typically celebrated as the achievement of a prodigious soloist, rather than that of the band that produced them. A boxed set of John Coltrane's quartet recordings was, for example, marketed as the work of a "heavyweight champion" of jazz rather than a series of "league champion" teams, even though twenty-two others played on the tracks therein (Coltrane, 1995). Such marketing overemphasises the role of the individual while marginalising the role of the group in the emergence of original work. Although the market value of a contemporary artwork depends on it being identified as the work of one inspired individual, the choices that shaped its physical and cultural emergence will inevitably have been driven by other people across the field of artistic commerce (Becker, 1984).

Multiple creative inputs into a valued piece of music are hard to conceptualise and quantify, as can be seen in the complexity of vituperative lawsuits over the rights to successful recordings (Kennedy,

2009). Nevertheless, while a group of people are improvising together, each makes their own choices about what should be played to some extent; and each choice made by each person has implications for what the others are playing. For instance, during a performance a drummer might choose to stop playing suddenly. In this event, the others will find the sound of their own instrument redefined, probably heard more prominently. If the drummer had been maintaining a regular pulse, each of the others may now choose to maintain it more or less clearly in what they play themselves; or to abandon the sense of pulse; or indeed to stop along with the drummer, further changing the sound of the ensemble. And each person in the group may choose differently.

This inherent unpredictability is what makes improvised music surprising and therefore creative, since it is bound to result in novel sounds and events. The creative quality is a property of the *group* rather than of any one member, and understanding it as a shared responsibility makes it potentially less daunting to the novice improviser. Many of those put off from improvising worry that they have not amassed the knowledge or abilities to imagine and execute a worthwhile piece of music, and therefore that their attempts will not be sufficiently creative. But it is easier to be involved in a group creative process where each person involved has a flexible scope to guide it. The decision that one person makes at a moment during an improvisation may not have the result they had foreseen—in fact, no one person may have a definitive overall perspective on what emerges—but each will inevitably have shaped that piece of music. In this sense, improvised group music may appear more creative than would something exercised by only one participant.

Yet if everyone involved in a free improvising group can make choices about what is played, there is a need to understand the following:

- if and how these choices are negotiated towards a creative goal

- how decisions can result in a performance that has not been seen or heard before
- how improvisers in that group can select from a vastly expanded array of possible acts on a moment-to-moment basis in order to take part meaningfully
- whether their creative processes share common principles with the ways in which idiomatic improvising takes place.

In the next section we describe research that addresses these lines of enquiry by examining the accounts of free improvisers.

Acting as an individual in an improvising group

As noted in chapter 2, psychological research has overwhelmingly considered musical improvisation as the behaviour of one individual, with a small body of work looking at how people improvise in pairs. To explore the far more common performance situation of playing in groups, we examined how some contemporary improvisers created music in this way (Wilson and MacDonald, 2016). Five trios were assembled through contacts known to the authors comprising individuals active in non-idiomatic improvised musical performance in the UK (e.g. Edinburgh-based improvising group Usurper pictured in Figure 4.1). Each group was invited to create an improvisation with no prior planning beyond the specification (for practical reasons) that it should be around five minutes long. The improvisations were audio and video recorded, with the option to repeat this process until a recording was reached to their satisfaction.[3]

Immediately after each recording, and before the performance could be discussed, each improviser was interviewed separately

[3] Examples of the music recorded are accessible at http://dx.doi.org/10.7488/ds/285.

Figure 4.1 Malcy Duff and Ali Robertson as improvising group Usurper, performing at Cafe Oto in London. Photo credit: Collette Robertson

about what had just taken place. They were shown the video recording of their group in sections of twenty seconds and asked after each by GW to describe the musical decisions that they and their fellow improvisers had made during that section. The interviews were analysed using grounded theory and discursive approaches. The improvisers' accounts suggest that, during the improvisation, each trio member evaluated the emerging music according to values they attributed to the group. The musical options they perceived to be open to them while playing could be grouped into a relatively small number of categories that followed a hierarchy of choices. These themes are described in subsequent sections.

Evaluating

Throughout the interviews, the improvisers were concerned with whether they liked what they or someone else was doing at a given point. When asked to explain what was happening during a piece, they described monitoring the overall texture as it unfolded (for instance the density, smoothness, or choppiness of sounds) or judging how satisfactorily the contributions of different players complemented each other. Novel or surprising elements were strongly favoured, but there were also concerns that the rate of innovation in the improvisation should be appropriate. This meant not becoming stagnant or relying on default practices, but also not being so unsettled as to lose coherence. One participant said:

> *It's so boring having pieces that start and they get louder and louder and crescendo and then they either stop or they get very crescendo and then they decrescendo and they fade out and it's so much crappy free improv that just does that basic shape, and it's just dull, generally.*

This went along with a desire for structure to emerge in what was played, highlighting that the music heard at a given moment is also evaluated in relation to what has gone before, and where it could be imagined to go. An improviser may, for instance, have a general liking for swirling runs of rapid notes. However, such playing may be evaluated as less desirable if the preceding three minutes have included little else, or if the group appears to be heading for a coordinated downbeat ending.

Maintaining or changing

Evaluation of what they heard informed the improvisers' choices of how to play. If an individual thought the music that was going on was satisfactory, intriguing, or enjoyable, or if they were not certain where it should go next, they might carry on with what they were currently doing. For instance, they might repeat a figure or rhythm; sustain a sound or sounds; keep emitting sporadic bursts of particular notes; or stay silent. Decisions like this accounted for most of what was played; as long as they evaluated the music positively, nothing substantively different was required. One participant said:

> *The fact that I'm just keeping that note there I knew at some point they would both be like "Ok he's going to do something in a minute." You keep that idea going and the chances are that at some point you're going to move away from it.*

The interviewees might, however, identify a need to contribute differently where they evaluated their trio's music negatively (for instance, as becoming too sparse or repetitive, or lacking a sense of development) or if it was perceived as transforming in some way. The primary decision arising from an improviser's ongoing evaluation of the music was therefore whether to *maintain* or *change* what they were doing. A decision to maintain required no further action than to keep evaluating. A decision to change, on the other hand, introduced further levels of choice.

Initiating or responding

Where it was felt that the music required change, an individual might decide to *initiate* a new direction in the music:

> *I remember that bit where it got noticeably louder being aware that, oh hello, things are a bit louder than often when I improvise . . . and I've maybe thought I could exert some control over it.*

At times, the improvisers described opting to play something unprecedented of their own devising. This could be to shake up what was going on, or to introduce novel possibilities for development: perhaps stopping suddenly, playing a new melody, or starting a rhythmic figure unrelated to what had gone before. Initiation of one's own new idea was immediately subject to evaluation; this decision was associated with a greater focus on self as the source of the new alternative, and asserted a dominant role for an improviser in the emerging music. It was reported relatively infrequently.

On the other hand, where an improviser heard the music transforming around them, or where they were struck by something played by one of the other members, they might change what they were doing in *response* to this. They still had to come up with something different to what they had been playing, but what they decided to change to was, to some extent, shaped or determined by the new musical context. The relationship between the musical environment and an individual's response to it defined three further categorisations of improvised response.

Responses: adopting, augmenting, or contrasting

Changes in an improviser's playing could be described as an adoption of what someone else was playing, for instance a repeated melodic or rhythmic figure, or a sound or pattern of sounds. *Adopting* what someone else was doing constituted acceptance of a new direction perceived in what others were playing, or a recognition that what someone else was doing was of interest and could be usefully emphasised to develop the music further. One participant said:

> *you can hear this sort of squeaky sound that I'm making, that's quite suggested from 1A's [object] squeaking, but then 1B's on it really quickly as well so we just all hit the squeakiness.*

At other times, improvisers described responding to what was being played elsewhere in the group by taking on some, but not all, aspects of what they heard. Rather than adopting another idea wholesale, an individual might decide to vary or *augment* another contribution, for instance by harmonising; by outlining some but not all beats or phrases within a rhythm; by outlining a different melodic contour; or by mimicking a texture with different timbre or varying volume. As one participant described:

> *it's just building that idea and throwing in a few more textual anomalies. In keeping with what the guitars had been doing previously, really, with the long harmonics and the "bup bup bup" sort of stuff.*

Finally, improvisers were sometimes prompted by what was being played elsewhere to provide *contrasting* material which was distinct from those sounds or represented an opposite sound, but which they saw as a meaningful accompaniment to that sound. If for example someone else was engaged in rapid cycles of notes, they might offer a sustained note, silence, or a repeated figure. If someone else played a string of long notes, they might decide to interrupt with short bursts of notes at unexpected intervals:

> *So she's providing the textures. We're providing the undercurrent of burbling nonsense underneath it.*

The categories and subcategories outlined in the previous sections were able to account for all the interviewees' explanations for what was played not just by themselves but also by the others in the group. This implies that the full gamut of options facing musicians when they improvise together can be represented by decisions to *maintain* or *change*; if changing, to *initiate* or *respond*; and if responding, to *augment, contrast*, or *adopt*.

Implications

Our findings suggest that most of the time improvising freely in a group is spent maintaining a musical idea for as long as this is evaluated as a good thing. The need for change is recognised only at intervals, according to that improviser's preferred rate of innovation. If the music is felt to require a new direction or development and this is not seen to be happening, the improviser will generate and execute a new idea if they can think of one and evaluate its impact. However, within a group of three or more, any individual is a minority. A change is more commonly prompted by what someone else in the group plays, or a revised evaluation of what someone else is doing. Perhaps, for instance, as a figure is repeated it becomes more noticeable to others (Deutsch, Henthorn, and Lapidis, 2011).

We understand the key choices for group improvisers—*maintaining, initiating, adopting, augmenting*, or *contrasting*—to be accessible through an expansion of the existing generative model for an individual jazz soloist (Johnson-Laird, 2002; Pressing, 1988). This expansion is represented in Figure 4.2.[4] While playing with others, an improviser is constantly cycling through an evaluative process. The salient differences are:

1. they may not be called on to generate (*initiate*) ideas at every iteration of this process, since much time may be spent in the top left corner of the diagram *maintaining* an existing idea.
2. generation of new ideas entirely by the individual is distinguished from generation of material in response to the ideas of others.

[4] After Wilson and MacDonald (2016). Musical choices during group free improvisation. *Psychology of Music*. *44*(5), 1029–1043 DOI:10.1177/0305735615606527.

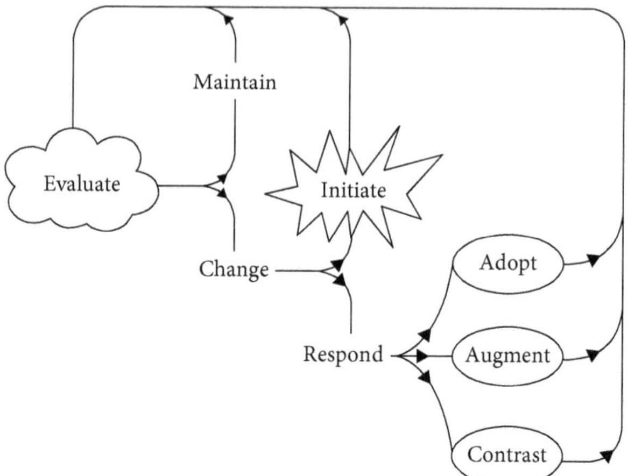

Figure 4.2 Model for the process of individual choice during group musical improvisation

Generative process

This model answers the questions raised earlier in this chapter. We understand that, in a freely improvised piece, individuals can imagine and execute something completely new to themselves as they play. The simultaneous divergent and convergent thinking that this feat requires should place extraordinary demands on their cognitive capacity (Canonne and Garnier, 2011), and doing so for the duration of a piece might be expected to be overwhelming. But in a group, improvisers are not necessarily generating new ideas on a moment-by-moment basis, or even for much of the time. They can instead spend relatively long periods executing one idea sustainedly, for as long as they feel it fits with what is going on around them (Figure 4.3).

In ambient drone improvisation produced by musicians such as Radu Malfatu, a sound may be maintained for almost the entirety of a piece (Arthurs, 2015). Even a truly solo improvisation will display passages of relatively constant or reiterating sounds. Most

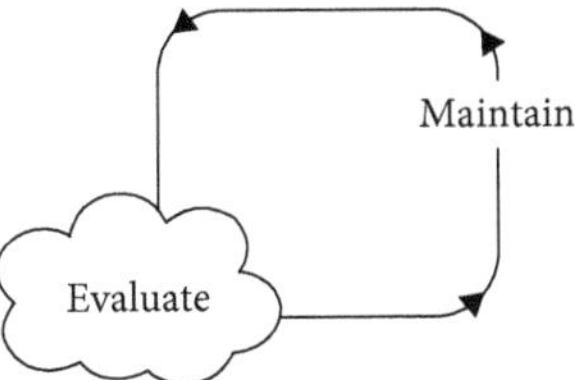

Figure 4.3 Maintain

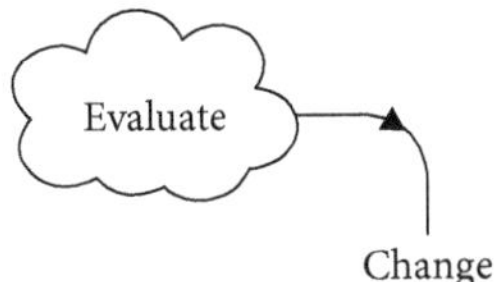

Figure 4.4 Change

music we play is characterised by recurring or sustained patterns, and such contributions to improvisation are therefore likely to be apprehended as musical, and thus ensemble improvising may require novelty from any one person only at a sporadic and variable rate. But one or more individuals will evaluate a need for a change from those maintained patterns at some point (Figure 4.4).

The improviser has more capacity for divergent thinking and an inward focus of attention while the music is in relative stasis between widely spaced changes. They have time to consider what they might like to initiate or introduce to the music in an original contribution (Figure 4.5).

If, however, change is prompted by an unpredicted act from another improviser, this period for consideration is not available to the same extent. The improviser can more readily access in the moment a response to what they hear by adopting, augmenting, or contrasting what someone else is playing (Figure 4.6) .

In this case their choices are constrained, not necessarily by the "rules" of a genre, but by what they hear, and the sense they make of

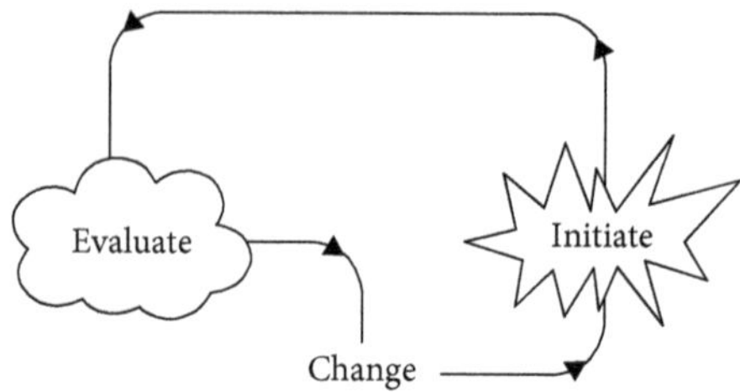

Figure 4.5 Initiate

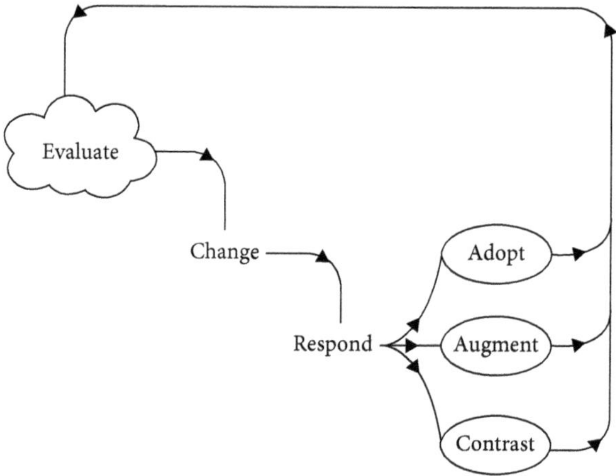

Figure 4.6 Respond

it. If one player introduces a new tempo or tonality, the others may change what they are doing but do not have to imagine a new tempo or tonality for themselves. If someone begins to play ascending notes, the others might adopt the same direction and rhythm; or play some of those notes but not all of them; or play a long tone to build tension as the notes climb. They are not summoning up independent ideas of what to play in a musical vacuum; rather, they are contributing to something that has already been suggested by others.

This narrowing of the pool of options goes some way to explaining how the cognitive demands of spontaneous novelty are met in an ensemble, where an improviser must also attend to what others are playing (Canonne and Garnier, 2011; Dietrich, 2004). There are constraints in such music, but rather than the stylistic constraints of a genre, these are essentially subjective and context-specific. They depend on the sense the individual player makes of what they hear at that moment, and of the social circumstances. If an individual considers their fellow improvisers to disdain tonally based improvising, they may choose to restrict themselves to atonal sounds on their instrument; playing a melody in such a context might risk appearing antagonistic.

This is consistent with recent findings from a study gathering images of the brain of a musician playing. Donnay et al. (2014) observed that regions associated with inhibition of individual ideas were more active when improvising with another musician outside the scanner than during a solo improvisation, in direct contrast to findings from the imaging of solo improvisers (Limb and Braun, 2008). When improvising with other people, we constrain ourselves accordingly. Framing group improvisation in terms of these choices also allows us to understand how material that is novel at a social or cultural level ("big-C" creativity, Sternberg, 2005) can emerge through improvisation. Initiating a new idea is perhaps closest to how we typically understand creativity in music: coming up with something that has novelty and value for the individual. However, each option to respond in a group improvisation can generate creative outcomes through interaction with other improvisers, rather than as one person's idea.

Augmentation represents a purposeful decision to vary what is currently being played. Improvised music may be transformed through a cycle of augmentations to an end that none of those involved could foresee, in the same way that a story or drawing may be transformed in sequential group paper-and-pen games such as *Consequences* or the Surrealists' *Exquisite Corpse* (Adamowicz, 1998).

Adoption can also foster unintended variation. If player B tries to adopt what player A is doing, they may accept as part of player A's contribution something that was not intended, for instance a fumbled note interpreted as an ornament. Accidental occurrences can in this way be converged upon or amplified as creative ideas. Furthermore, player B may not immediately succeed in mimicking player A perfectly—if they play a different instrument, this will be all but impossible. Therefore, although B may have intended to play exactly what A did, what emerges may represent a transformation of A's contribution. Player A may in turn perceive this as a divergent idea.

Finally, if player B offers a *contrast*—for instance, a regularly repeated chord while player A contributes sporadic flurries of notes—they may intend this to offset what A is doing. Player A may, however, decide that B has proposed a new idea and stop playing to make way for this. In this scenario, the music that emerges from their combined playing will not be what either player had themselves imagined.

To summarise, our model displays a hierarchical process of choice with five endpoints or outcomes that can be directly evaluated in a return to the start of the process: maintain, initiate, adopt, augment, or contrast. Of these, maintaining is a passive choice, while the other four constitute actions (Figure 4.7). An individual improviser choosing to change will understand themselves to be taking one of those four options. But any other member of their group (or audience) may understand them to be taking one of the other paths, and react accordingly. This potential for *mis*understanding is the creative engine of group improvisation. By circumventing individual intentions and embracing noise in the system, unprecedented outcomes can be reached.

In real time, choices may have to be made with little conscious reflection. Expressionist artists sought to capitalise on the exigencies

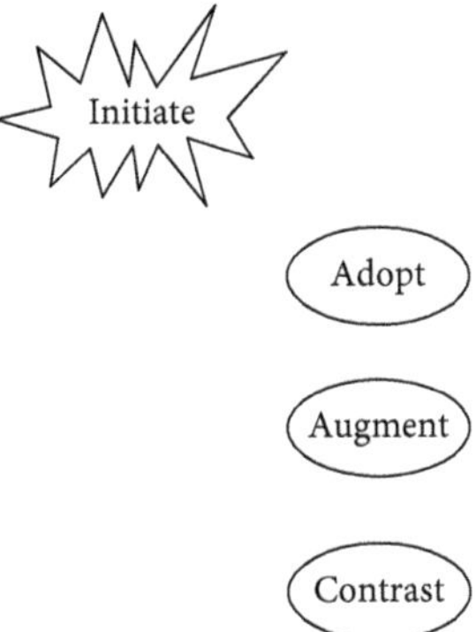

Figure 4.7 Active outcomes—initiate, adopt, augment, contrast

of automatic drawing, seeing "accidents" when drawing rapidly as producing something more interesting than work created consciously or with time for reflection (Barron, Dube, and Palazzo Grassi, 1997). This is reflected in the experiences that some of our interviewees have described, of the music taking on "a life of its own," or of improvisation as a mysterious, instinctive process (Wilson and MacDonald 2005; Wilson and MacDonald 2016). They sensed at some points that music was developing, but could not identify themselves or any one member of the band as steering this development.

Cochrane (2017), defining such instances in terms of group flow as "cognitively distributed tasks," suggests that each individual musician's intention is formed in relation to an external musical product arising socially from the whole group. However, improvisers in a group may not experience the formation of clear intentions (Hart and Di Blasi, 2013). Our findings suggest further that for a group improvisation to be not only social but also creative, that product *must* be apprehended in different ways by each member. Novelty emerges explicitly through interaction and the mismatch of intentions, rather than through individual initiatives.

Because this process is beyond individual control, the constraints of a genre cannot readily be enforced.

This is not to argue that traditional learned skills and knowledge have no place in improvisation; these options can be exercised with or without such constraints. Achieving something through this process that has value for an audience (something that other people will commit time and money to come and hear) may require the accumulation of particular knowledge and skills, and these will always be required for improvisation to be recognisable within a specific genre. For instance, production of a figured bass line within the baroque keyboard tradition will require familiarity with how others have done so in the past, and the skill of improvising with one hand while playing a written melody in the other (Bailey, 1993). A baroque player still has the option in any performance to lean their forearm suddenly on the keyboard instead, or reverse what their hands are doing as a creative gesture, if they feel like doing so. They learn to constrain themselves from doing so to meet the expectations of audiences and other players of a particular musical style.

However, processes are still creative if they have value at an individual level. Parents and grandparents may be hugely excited by a baby's improvised vocalisations, even if these sounds would not impress a wider concert-going audience to the same extent. Our model therefore suggests that the choices made by an improviser in *any* group setting are comparable, whether or not they are commercially viable or artistically laudable. This means that, although derived from observation of free improvising, the model applies to improvised activity in any genre or domain.

In free non-idiomatic music, all players are usually assumed to have equivalent remit and can make the choices we have set out as they please; they may for instance devote more time to maintaining and evaluating than improvisers in other forms would. In other music, particular roles (according to instrument, status, or the requirements of the genre) shape the types of input that improvisers can choose, or the routes through our model that they prioritise.

A frontline jazz "soloist" such as a saxophonist is expected primarily to initiate ideas, and generally to avoid repeating or sustaining a sound. To varying degrees, those playing accompanying instruments (such as drummers) must maintain a pulse, adopt or augment elements of what the soloist plays, or provide contrasting elements such as a pedal point. For that reason, a bass player who has not learned to improvise fast walking bass lines might not be hired for a band in a jazz club, but that does not mean that they are unable to improvise or interact creatively through music in some form. What is important to recognise is that all are still making decisions as they go, not just the person in front of the group.

Working with the model

The model represented in Figure 4.2 was developed by listening to what improvisers said they were doing when they played, and locates the key decisions described by improvisers within a cyclical process. It therefore draws on conscious and retrospective accounts of how they went about improvising that were delivered while watching themselves on video, a standpoint they did not have while playing. Like other improvisers we have spoken to, they stressed that it felt difficult or unusual to try to put this process into words. In the course of playing, decisions may be made so fast that they are not conscious choices, and an internal representation of something that would be good to play is formed and executed almost instantaneously. What the improvisers' words give us is an insider's post hoc account of why each act must have happened. Nevertheless, this model suggests that an individual within a group who follows this process, at whatever level of skill and knowledge they have, will find themselves functioning as an improviser.

We have tested this proposition by treating the model as a score for group improvisation under the working title *Stones, Clouds*. Trying to improvise with each other through conscious decisions to maintain, initiate, adopt, augment, or contrast highlighted that the decisions of musical improvisers are pre-verbal. We therefore sought to represent the categories of choice visually, first as an array of stones of different qualities that one could imagine picking up. At a subsequent performance for the Concurrent research network,[5] collaboration with improvisers from dance and visual art required the model to be presented in three-dimensional objects amongst which the improvisation could take place. Visual artist Cath Keay designed a series of cloud-like forms to represent each of the categories of choice.[6] The sculptures were arrayed in the performance space as a visual score (Figure 4.8).

The instructions for the score were to start playing (or dancing or drawing) and thereafter to execute any of the choices that led back to evaluation: maintaining; initiating a new idea; or adopting, augmenting, or contrasting what someone else is doing. Afterwards, some of those involved gave us their reflections in the process in an interview. What struck us, as well as everyone we have asked to improvise using only these options, is that it felt very unnatural to make such choices consciously. Most people report that, sooner or later, they find themselves responding instinctively to the improvisation around them, without thinking first about which option they will take. This is consistent with neuroscientific and other research suggesting that many of the practices of improvisation are facilitated by subconscious processes (Beaty, 2015). But in all other respects exercising only those choices felt to them, and looked to an audience, like improvisation.

In subsequent workshops based on this score (Wilson and MacDonald, 2019) we have asked a range of improvisers first to practice *maintaining*; then *adopting*; then *augmenting*; then *contrasting*. When they are then asked to perform together using

[5] https://vimeo.com/174818620

[6] These were based on the Expressionist works of Wenzel Hablik, an artist preoccupied with the spontaneous generation of form (Whyte, 1985).

Figure 4.8 Ana Almeida and Una MacGlone performing in *Stones, Clouds* at Concurrent#1, University of Edinburgh, 2015. Sculpture by Cath Keay. Photo credit: Full Zoom Photography

only those four options consciously and whenever they choose, participants still tend to report that what they are doing is improvising. This is the case even though they have not been asked explicitly to "improvise," and even though the option of initiating has not been included. In other words, people can feel that they are improvising together even if none of them is seeking to take the initiative with new ideas entirely from their own imagination, even if they are only working with sounds, movements, or images that are already present in the piece.

This practical work confirms and underscores what we conclude from our empirical research described previously, that creativity within group improvisation occurs at a level beyond the individual through the interaction of choices that are largely responsive rather than generative in themselves. In video recordings of *Stones, Clouds,* performances can be seen to evolve and develop. One player may adopt another's pattern and maintain it after that other has stopped doing so. Meanwhile, someone else provides contrasting random stabs that become a new theme as others in turn adopt or augment them. This new work cannot be fully apprehended or predicted from the perspective of any one individual, and they may all feel that what emerges is primarily someone else's idea. Nevertheless, through each improviser being selective about what to respond to and how, the emergent work can represent their tastes and beliefs as an ensemble; it will have value for them, and for a relevant audience.

There are two important senses in which our model can form the foundation of an inclusive approach to improvisation and music making in general. When someone picks up a guitar for the first time, they may be a long way from being able to execute "Stairway to Heaven" as in the original. But they can improvise with the instrument there and then by experimenting with the options in our model: see what sound it makes (initiate), try to keep that sound going (maintain), try to play some or all of what they can hear someone else do (augment or adopt), or deliberately try to make a different sound (contrast). This will be a creative act in a way that reproducing "Stairway to Heaven" (yet again) would not be, since something unforeseen will come of it. If they act in this way simultaneously with another individual, whatever that individual's abilities, the result is likely to go beyond whatever either of them may have envisaged playing. In fact, the increased likelihood of contributions being adopted *in*accurately will make the resulting music even more unpredictable, even more likely to generate novelty.

That novel outcome may or may not have commercial or aesthetic value in culture at large. But it may have therapeutic value within a music therapy session, or personal value in being exciting, amusing, or dramatic. It may be educationally valuable as a step towards that individual understanding what music can do for them and what they might achieve in the future, expanding the range of musical possibilities they can imagine in a way that a familiar instrument could not. For saxophonist Ornette Coleman, taking up the violin left-handed in mid-career expanded what he could contribute to an improvisation, whether or not he might have held down a chair in an orchestral string section. Novice or student improvisers may reach a clearer understanding of their own objectives and of how to get the most from interacting with other improvisers if they are encouraged to try responding to other improvisers and to reflect on how that was valuable to them. Basing their participation on responses to others may also seem less daunting than feeling they have to bring an individual vision to life.

Even if someone does not feel comfortable with generating spontaneous alternatives throughout a piece, or is put off doing so by the conviction that their ideas would lack wider value, they may still engage in a creative process as part of a group by adopting and seeking to maintain elements of other players' ideas that they do feel comfortable with.

This chapter has highlighted the importance of group interaction in the creative processes of improvisation. It has reached the following conclusions:

- Improvisation can be considered most creative when it transcends social or cultural expectations, but such achievements are not explained if improvisers base their choices on what they know and have internalised.
- Because group improvisation involves multiple simultaneous choices, outcomes are not predictable from any individual choice, and improvisation is more likely to innovate at a group or higher level.
- Our model identifies key categories of decision made by members of a group including whether or not to change; whether to initiate or respond; and what kind of response to give.

- These allow improvisation at any level to become novel and valuable in particular ways; new directions are generated through the interplay of choices, none of which may have been intended to lead to that outcome.
- Approaching improvisation with this understanding can enhance improvised interaction in new ways, for instance between performers from different disciplines.

In the next chapter, we consider how choices are understood between improvisers.

5
Distributed creativity and the myth of shared understanding

Improvisation often appears telepathic. In one of many video clips he has uploaded to the internet,[1] American pianist Dotan Negrin is sitting at a piano on a Paris street playing round a cycle of chords when an older passerby asks if he can join him. Without Negrin breaking stride, the newcomer begins to improvise melodic lines further up the keyboard, around the chords being played. After a while, he moves round behind Negrin to start playing the same chord sequence himself, further down the keyboard, using his own voicings and rhythms but again without breaking the tempo. Negrin now begins to improvise melodic lines around what the newcomer is playing. At a certain point the two simultaneously begin to play in a heavily accented rhythm of regular triplets.

It turns out that the newcomer is Danish pianist and composer Frans Bak. The potential for two musicians from separate countries to meet by chance for the first time in a foreign street is highly coincidental. To do so while playing, and to immediately and spontaneously create unprecedented and appealing music without prior discussion, is remarkable enough to have propelled this clip to over a million views. How, for instance, are they able suddenly to coordinate a shift of the rhythmic emphasis from four beats to twelve without even looking up?

It might be assumed that this is possible because, as two knowledgeable improvisers, each can understand what the other plays,

[1] https://www.youtube.com/watch?v=Nsn8ZGb80-g

The Art of Becoming. Raymond A. R. MacDonald and Graeme B. Wilson, Oxford University Press (2020).

DOI: 10.1093/oso/9780190840914.001.0001

anticipate how that person will continue to play, and that their pianistic training and experience allow them to execute what constitutes an appropriate accompaniment or response. Yet cultural differences between the environments where these two men are likely to have learned to play should lead inevitably to differences of taste, training, and musical values. It seems unlikely that they could have acquired exactly the same set of ideas and abilities. Furthermore, they know at the outset nothing more about each other than what they can see. How can they form workable ideas of someone else's musical intentions with such limited information?

Research on improvisation tends to assume that in a successful group performance, musicians must have the same conception of the quality and meaning of the music they play. While chapter 4 focused on individual accounts of improvising, this chapter will compare the accounts of different improvisers within a group, to reach an explanation of whether and how these are negotiated while playing together. We critique the assumption that improvisers must share understanding of what they are trying to achieve and how they should do so, and demonstrate that improvisation can take place to participants' satisfaction in the absence of their shared understanding. Finally, we suggest that what is necessary instead is for participants to feel invested in the group process.

Comparing the understandings of improvisers within a group

When we play music together, we like to feel that we are working together. The experience of being lost in a folk tune, or unable to play one's part in an orchestra, is uncomfortable and isolating because it exposes us as being adrift from everyone else, or not having learned the piece as well as others. This is no less the case when we improvise music with other people. For instance, someone coming from the European music tradition needs to know where a tune starts, or where the first beat falls. This can leave them disoriented if trying to play along with West African drummers who do not frame what they play in the same way (Smith, Viljoen, and McGeachie, 2014). Nevertheless, the idea that unfamiliar musicians can meet for the first time and improvise together is popular. After-hours clubs at festivals, for instance, are receptive to the idea of visitors "sitting in" on a performance.

If we expect a group improvisation to be unpredictable and to be created through interaction as it is played, why should any one player expect to know where they are relative to the others, or expect that others are thinking what they are thinking? A popular explanation is that improvisers who have never met will nevertheless have amassed knowledge, skills, and approaches that are recognisable to each other (Canonne and Aucouturier, 2016; Monson, 1996). The extensive literature on jazz pedagogy prioritises "paying dues" before becoming an improviser. This implies that, to sit in with a band in a strange town (and hence pick up work), one must have learnt a repertory of melodies, rhythms, phrases, and theoretical rules which that band are also likely to know. This allows one to understand their music as it emerges, rather than feeling like an outsider.

Psychological studies have explored the idea of shared understanding within a tradition. Researchers have analysed the materials executed by individual soloists (e.g., Schütz, 2012) or solo improvisers (e.g., Norgaard, 2011, 2014) for recurring elements consistent with the jazz tradition. It is argued that these recurring elements are recognisable to others active in the same field. Yet improvised interaction is possible for infants or for music therapy clients who bring no musical learning to the task. Improvisation with a stranger is therefore possible without having spent time acquiring musical proficiency or precise control of an instrument. In fact, even individuals with specialist knowledge and skills in the same field may diverge in their understanding of playing together.

Schober and Spiro (2014) empirically tested the degree of shared understanding between improvisers. They asked a pianist and a saxophonist active in New York's jazz scene to arrive in a studio from either side of a dividing screen, and perform a familiar jazz standard together. The musicians were then asked in separate interviews to evaluate their recorded performance. It was expected that, being active in the same professional jazz scene, they would share a close understanding of the performance and therefore rate all the evaluative statements similarly after some weeks. They found instead that the two musicians' answers corresponded little better than if they had filled in the questionnaire at random. These expert jazz musicians came away from improvising together with divergent ideas about what they had just played together. The saxophonist's explanation for his answers, moreover, indicate that he did not necessarily expect complete consistency of outlook. For him, the nature of artistic creativity meant that he wanted interaction to throw up surprises, unpredictable events, otherwise his practice might stagnate. He therefore did not expect that both musicians *would* apprehend such surprises in the same way.

Research evidence, then, has pointed to reliance on familiar material when improvising a "solo" either literally or within a group, but also to divergence in how improvisers appraise what they are playing together.

Social construction of meaning in music and language

The presumption of shared understanding between improvisers is consistent with the popular discourse of music as a language within which improvisation takes place (Monson, 1996). Music is, furthermore, sometimes characterised as a *universal* language for improvisation, going beyond the cultural limits of verbal languages. We accept that to communicate in another country, an effort must be made to learn some vocabulary and grammar of the tongue spoken there; in drama, actors who do not share some language can improvise together only with gesture. In recent years, however, some celebrated music has been improvised between individuals from radically different musical backgrounds. Improvisers in Indian classical music, for instance, spend many years assimilating a lexicon of patterns and practising combining and recombining them (Paranjape, 2012). Yet striking fusion music has taken place with musicians from outwith this tradition; to play with Anoushka Shankar, jazz pianist Herbie Hancock cannot have acquired her familiarity since childhood with the practices of a sitarist.

It might be argued instead that musical improvisers from different traditions will have internalised musical elements whose harmonic or rhythmic structure can be meaningfully or pleasingly mapped onto each other, so that each can understand what the other is doing and integrate their styles. This is to underplay the novelty that is valued in these meetings: the surprise of hearing a blues riff over the urgent delicacy of a tabla, and the idea that unfamiliar territory is being negotiated in real time, for the first time. We might consider improvisation less in terms of what knowledge and skills are shared between improvisers, and more in terms of how their ideas and assumptions diverge. It is the musical negotiation that creates breakthrough moments of wonder, excitement, and innovation; this negotiation takes place in real time with perhaps some shared knowledge but inevitably significant differences in musical backgrounds.

Social constructionist theory, as discussed in chapter 3, holds that language cannot refer only to objective meanings with universal interpretations. A statement such as "I want to play the guitar one day" unavoidably invokes a wider range of possible meanings depending where it is made and by who. Spoken in a bassoon lesson, a gamelan rehearsal, or a totalitarian society, these words may be interpreted as rejection of establishment music, of a cultural heritage, or of ideological compliance. They may be received by a teacher as an aspiration to be encouraged; by a friend as an assertion of musical identity; or by a parent as an appeal for expenditure on what may be a fad. If an adult is on stage with a guitar in their hand, the same words may even function as an ironic joke.

In making the statement, the speaker implies characteristics both for themselves (e.g., as someone deserving to play the instrument) and for others (e.g., as someone who has inspired this desire). A listener's interpretation will depend on their personal understandings of the speaker, where they are speaking, and in whose presence. They may take different meanings from those words next time they hear them. Knowledge of English definitions and grammar alone are insufficient to access these myriad shades of meaning. Yet conversations do not break down through uncertainty because everyone present makes different sense of what is said. As long as each person is able to make sense for themselves within the immediate context of what is said, they can carry on taking part.

By way of illustration: in 2006 a job interviewee arriving at the BBC was mistakenly ushered onto a news programme to be interviewed as an expert commentator (Fisher, 2010). In the broadcast, the first question clearly reveals to the interviewee that he is the victim of mistaken identity; his understanding of the context and the questions he faces is immediately transformed. He conforms to this understanding by answering as best he can. This in turn allows the interviewer to carry on quizzing him despite making completely different sense of the interview. Their exchange is thus *generated* by misunderstanding: he might not have answered as he did if he believed himself to be in a job interview, while she would not have engaged with his volunteered opinions if she had realised his lack of expertise. Yet the programme did not suddenly collapse; the interview proceeded to completion with no recognition from the on-air team of the error made.[2]

Our argument here, in line with the principles of social constructionism, is that the sharing of understanding between

[2] https://www.youtube.com/watch?v=e6Y2uQn_wvc.

participants is no more necessary in improvisation than it is for such a conversation to take place. Furthermore, the unique aspects of musical communication mean that performers' different understandings of the same improvised moment can produce music that musicians and audiences regard as revelatory.

Unshared understandings of improvisation: research evidence

Conversations and group improvisations are both creative social processes, continuing as long as they generate novel material that is of value or interest to those involved. The comparison to language made in the previous section suggests that musical improvisation can take place even though each participant's unique experiences must give them a distinct perspective on any sound that emerges; and even if lack of expertise dysfluency, or unfamiliarity gives each participant a radically different grasp of what is taking place. A social constructionist understanding of interaction during improvisation would be that

> every sound or silence fielded has implications within that context for its originator and for each of those hearing it; the implications perceived by these individuals may coincide to a greater or lesser degree, or not at all, whatever their previous shared experience. (Wilson and MacDonald, 2017)

We carried out a qualitative study of members of an ensemble that explicitly brought together musicians from different backgrounds to improvise together. Glasgow Improvisers Orchestra (GIO) has included members who are relatively well-known musicians from pop or indie bands, the Scottish folk scene, jazz, and classical music. Despite this profusion of idioms represented, the ensemble's improvising is essentially non-idiomatic in that no conventions of these different genres are observed. As fellow members of this ensemble, we conducted separate in-depth interviews with ten of these individuals to examine how they thought about their improvising together, relative to their diverse musical training and acculturation; and to consider the extent to which they shared understanding of each other's choices (Wilson and MacDonald, 2012).

Our analysis showed that interviewees oriented towards a shared group identity. By framing many of the improvising practices within the ensemble as something "we" do, they proposed ways of playing together that were accessible to everyone in the ensemble. There were nevertheless distinct differences in how they prioritised these capacities. As previously observed in our studies of jazz musicians, improvising in GIO was sometimes seen to depend on acquired expertise in traditional skills and knowledge, one interviewee for instance asserting that "we're all highly skilled on our instruments." But elsewhere, musical naïveté was proposed as something that heightened the capacity for novelty and thus creativity. Not being able to recognise or execute particular scales or chords, for instance, meant that something more instinctive, personal, and unforeseen was likely to emerge.

Some of the interviewees referred to a specific event within one GIO improvisation. On that occasion, many members of the ensemble had fallen silent during the piece while others continued to play. While each interviewee recognised this event as a moment of simultaneous choice for silence, they offered divergent understandings of why people had made that choice. One musician recalled falling silent because it was musically appropriate for fewer people to play at that point, explaining

> *if there's something that you think should be there you should do it. Well what I thought should be there is less of everything.*

Another suggested that others' choice of silence was due to uncertainty or nerves:

> *I think a lot of them felt inhibited.*

A third treated others' silence as an expression of disapproval, in which context she felt unable to play herself:

> *if I think that something's really nice and I see someone being kind of grrrr in the corner it really it puts me off, I just can't, I have to stop.*

These distinct explanations each construct various characteristics for the interviewee and their fellow improvisers: for instance, being more or less experienced, authoritative, confident, aggressive, or sensitive.

This demonstrates that musical meanings of improvised events can be shaped by social construction in the same way as verbal meanings in conversation. It therefore makes little sense to assume that improvisers must understand their interaction in the same terms; they will inevitably bring contrasting shades of understanding to what they play together.

How meaning is socially constructed in improvisation

In our study of trios that identified improvisers' options of *maintaining*, *initiating* change, or *responding* (*adopting*, *augmenting*, or *contrasting*), we also assessed how routine or unusual it was for their understandings to diverge (Wilson and MacDonald, 2017). As well as analysing how participants accounted for their own choices, we examined how those choices were supported by characterisations of other members of the trio. During the interviews, the video recordings were replayed for discussion twenty seconds at a time. This allowed different members' descriptions of particular musical events to be compared, along with their reasoning for why the event had taken place. In keeping with qualitative methodology, our intention was not to count the number of instances that could be labelled as shared or not shared, but to identify whether understandings could diverge, and to understand what musical features might be associated with this ambiguity. We also wanted to consider whether trio members treated their version of events as shared by the others, and what they thought would confirm this.

Convergence and divergence

The trio members' accounts converged around some events and diverged around others. Where all three members of a group offered the same version of an episode, this tended to be an observation that everyone in the group was *maintaining* what they were playing. Thus, shared understanding seemed feasible at a time when sounds or textures were sustained rather than changing rapidly or suddenly. Even where the group concurred that everyone was maintaining sounds, individuals might perceive distinct reasons for this choice: for instance, everyone enjoying the texture of sounds as they were, or waiting for an appropriate moment to change, or feeling uncertain and therefore biding one's time.

Some passages of *change* also elicited strongly similar accounts of who had initiated and how others had responded to this. For instance, in one improvisation there was a sudden change across the trio from a quiet ongoing pattern to a texture of strident clashing sounds. In their interviews, all three trio members identified that the pianist had instigated this change because she had felt the music needed more, and saw the other two instrumentalists as "going with her" by adopting the same sound texture.

However, passages where the music changed substantially were more often described differently by different individuals taking part. For example:

- one person in a trio saw a texture being created through the concerted efforts of all three members
- another member considered only herself to be responding to someone else's choices
- the third saw all players' input as unrelated, with each having a different idea about the music: "three different thoughts going on at once."

Even if a trio agreed that a change had occurred, their understandings of whose choice it had been could be contradictory. Two different members of a trio might each think they had instigated a change for their own reason, or might each give different versions of who had been responding to whom. Changes were sometimes described by all three members of a trio as having been someone else's initiative.

It might be argued that the improvisations had "gone wrong" if participants understood them so differently. However, all trios agreed that the improvisations they recorded were a reasonable representation of their usual practice; and whether or not the rest of the group shared their understanding at these points, participants had carried on improvising, confident with their idea of what the others were trying to do. Some participants commented directly on whether understandings were, or needed to be, shared among the group. Sometimes they expressed certainty that fellow trio members felt the same way they did, with decisions reported in the first-person plural ("we're letting it build," etc.).

However, at other times, interviewees suggested they could not understand what others were doing or thinking. Some stated further that they did not expect to understand what everybody intended. One stated that the music would be too predictable if

Figure 5.1 Noizechoir, Newcastle upon Tyne. Photo credit: Noizechoir

everyone understood each other's decisions perfectly, and the unpredictability of the music was what he valued. Participants talked of the music at certain points as being driven or shaped by itself, rather than by the deliberate decisions of any member of the group.

These findings indicate that improvisers can successfully create music together in which all are invested, while maintaining diverse understandings of what they are all doing and why. The UK group Noizechoir (Figure 5.1) specialise in vocal improvising while celebrating diverse backgrounds, approaches, and understandings of improvisational processes. Similarly, Malachi Favors, from The Art Ensemble of Chicago (Figure 5.2), was an original member of the Association for the Advancement of Creative Musicians (AACM) in Chicago. The AACM is an organisation, with global influence, founded to enhance the careers of African American musicians while embracing a truly eclectic approach to composition and improvisation (Lewis, 2002).

Figure 5.2 Malachi Favors at the 1999 Glasgow International Jazz Festival. Photo credit: Robert Burns

Identities within a group

The preceding claim does not imply that our participants took no account of who they were improvising with. In discussing how their fellow improvisers had played, they constructed particular versions of each other. They ascribed certain musical preferences or values to their fellow players, such as liking folk music, particular chord voicings, or the style of other artists, or avoiding recognisable rhythms. These expectations were backed up with reference to how that person had played on previous occasions, or tastes they had previously expressed.

Assumptions about fellow improvisers emerged as both a limit on choice and as a resource for improvising. Things that an interviewee might have decided to play (e.g., regular rhythms) were selected or avoided depending on how fellow trio members were expected to react to or recognise them. Colleagues' playing could be interpreted as referring to something played or discussed together in the past. Familiarity was therefore repeatedly invoked as influential on musical interactions. Nevertheless, when trio members' accounts were compared, it was not obvious that attempts to communicate familiar material were consistently received, or that material was reliably familiar across the group.

For instance, one participant had deliberately played part of a tune by the other two trio members, who made no mention of this in their interviews when discussing the same passage. It may be that they did not feel it was worth communicating to the interviewer that they recognised their own tune. However, it was also apparent that passages could be hailed by different trio members as referring to completely separate occasions. One interviewee, for instance, maintained that a particular combination of sounds was familiar from a graphic score that all three trio members had performed before. Another member of the trio took this passage as a clear reference to an entirely different piece from their shared back catalogue.

The difficulty of improvising with less familiar people was a recurring theme. In each ensemble, one member was less used to playing with the other two than they were with each other. In each trio, the pair who were more familiar regarded this "wild card" as less predictable, requiring greater attention when the group played together. This implied a level of trust or confidence in what a familiar improviser might do; vocalists in particular emphasised that it was vital for them to feel they could trust their fellow improvisers to accept whatever decisions they made.

A sense of familiarity therefore emerged as a significant means to build the trust necessary to improvise together, even if that trust did not correspond to an apparent shared understanding.

Conclusions and implications

These data refute in several ways the idea that, in order to improvise together, improvisers need to understand exactly what each other is doing, or to respond predictably to what someone else plays. We have observed that

- Social construction of improvised events means that we cannot assume that improvisers must understand their interaction in the same terms.
- While members of an ensemble might recognise some of what they improvise in consistent ways, their understandings tend to diverge as the music changes.
- Even if understandings diverge, improvisers may expect that others attach similar meanings to events, and can perceive improvising as working if they can make their own sense of it and experience trust.
- Their explanations of what the group is doing depend on how they construct their fellow improvisers.
- Improvisers who are familiar with each other expect this to influence their improvising together, but their expectations or recognitions may not match with each other.
- A lack of shared understanding, or an inability to tell who is driving changes at some points, may also be valued as means to achieve surprising results when improvising.

The findings underline the importance of investigating improvisation by more than two people, given that most improvisation takes place at this ensemble level. Comparing different members' accounts of an event within an ensemble improvisation adds to the insight from Schober and Spiro's study (2014), which considered only whether players within a duo agreed on evaluative statements that did not necessarily refer to the same occurrence. Seasoned practitioners are likely to attest to mastery of a shared body of knowledge and skills, and therefore understanding, as a necessary prerequisite for improvising in groups (Wilson and MacDonald, 2005). With this perspective it may appear counterintuitive to suggest that improvisation can take place without a common understanding between those involved. However, as Schober and Spiro suggest in response to their findings, understanding between improvisers may best be viewed as existing on a continuum.

We undoubtedly found members of a group giving closely similar accounts of what each person in the group was doing, and why, at certain points. Many years of teaching and learning are spent trying to build confidence in being able to "read" and respond to any improvising situation in ways that one's collaborators should expect.

Nevertheless, the divergence in accounts that was more obvious at times of change did not cause the improvising to break down. What should be recognised, though, is that it did appear important to individuals that they *felt* they could make sense of what others were doing—that they could trust their own judgements, and could trust others to be making sense of them as well. Although improvisers may expect to share understanding, this may not be as important as believing that shared understanding exists. As long as each person *thinks* that they are working together, their interaction will show musical qualities.

Psychology researchers are beginning to focus on free improvisation as a testing ground for models of improvised musical interaction, or as a form of improvising in which performers have the greatest scope for creative choices. It has been suggested that free improvisers' mental models of improvising may become more similar the more they engage in this practice (Canonne and Aucouturier, 2016; Canonne and Garnier, 2011). However, rather than a universal or objective knowledge that can be learnt, our findings point more towards the emergence over time of idiosyncratic musical acts that have personal meaning when played with someone familiar: what saxophonist Evan Parker has labelled "tropes," that accumulate between improvisers who play together repeatedly over a period of time (Smith, 2013). Although those who play together repeatedly may find that similar events recur in their collaboration, those tropes are a phenomenon arising from the group but will not necessarily be consistently understood among them.

If two improvisers have played together on many previous occasions, certain options that one of them might take—spinning a metal ball or making tiny "lip noises" in the case of our participants—will have particular meaning for that person in the context of the duo's history. Those options may also mean something to the other person who has heard these sounds before. Each may take their appearance as implying that the improvisation is now going somewhere in particular. But if the pair have never talked about the meaning of these sounds, and associate them with different occasions, they might recognise them as having distinct implications from the "Rolodex" of memories referred to by one interviewee, and therefore decide on different courses of action at any point. They are, then, individually meaningful, and individuals might consider them meaningful at a group level. However, they cannot be assumed to hold consistent associations for the group. In this way a recurring pattern of improvisation can manifest between regularly collaborating improvisers without being interpreted the same way by each person on each occasion.

"Tropes," then, may not represent permanent associations laid down in the memory of those who have come to recognise them. The ways in which trio members in our study accounted for their group's improvising were strongly consistent with the processes of social construction described earlier in this chapter. When an individual described a choice made by someone in the ensemble, they rationalised it in terms of a particular version of the people in that particular social context. That musical contribution might in turn be interpreted by someone else in the group as having potentially different implications depending on how they understood themselves, others, and the situation. Meanings attached to music were thus personal, flexible, and context-dependent, in the same way that verbal utterances in a conversation ascribe certain characteristics to the speaker and their listeners. If they were to play or hear that sound in another context, for instance with different musicians or on stage in front of an audience, it might mean something different.

This argument suggests that although sound practices may acquire particular association for a group of musicians who encounter them together over a period of time, they will not only be personal to each musician (i.e., different individuals may recognise a trope but have different ways of constructing it), but they may change in response to context. This may be either the immediate musical context (having different associations at a moment of silence or as an opening gambit); the temporal context (e.g., losing this novelty over time and coming to be seen as annoying rather than comforting); or the immediate social context (two people may share a musical in-joke, but if a third person is playing with them, it acquires a separate resonance). In social constructionist terms, tropes represent a repertoire of musical associations unique to an established group of improvisers, and importantly, one which is subject to variation and reshaping depending on context.

However, it was argued earlier in this chapter that creative innovations, the surprising outcomes of group improvisation that can transform or transcend expectations of what is aesthetic or possible, are in many respects the most valued qualities of the music. It might be argued that by the time a practice has become recognisable within a group as a trope, it has lost some of its capacity for innovative use. Tropes might best be seen as something like a group genre; through repeated use and habituation, certain practices become entrenched, characterising what that group does and constraining expectations in the same way that culturally accessible expectations of Indian classical music or rock and roll make us anticipate particular musical acts from sitars or guitars in those genres. How then can true innovations in practice come about through improvising? The development of tropes of practice between improvisers can only be part of the global process.

The study reported in this chapter and chapter 4 employed qualitative methods appropriate to our aim to develop theory, and therefore gathered very rich data from a smaller sample size than would quantitative research aiming to find statistically significant differences in one characteristic. Through detailed analysis we arrived at an explanation consistent with all views expressed, rather than a hypothesised proportion of our sample, and can therefore be confident of the generalisability of our findings to wider genres and populations of improvisers (Banister, Burman, Parker, Taylor, and Tindall, 1998). Further research with such groups is likely to enrich rather than refute what we have argued.

Our findings suggest that misunderstandings between improvisers might lead to unexpected events and responses within group improvisation. Improvisers arrive at different understandings of what is going on from those of their fellow improvisers, so that when they respond on the basis of that understanding, they are therefore more likely to surprise the others. If a series of responses that are not understood by others builds up or becomes concatenated, it seems likely that the music will be perceived as having its own momentum, or "driving itself," since other members of the ensemble do not appear to be making the choices that are anticipated. So, although improvisers may feel that they share understanding, that feeling or belief in shared understanding may be more important to what they are doing than whether or not they actually do share understanding. As long as each person in an improvising group thinks that they are working together, their interaction will show musical qualities. Trust and commitment to the musical and social interaction are key to its success, rather than shared understanding.

Two implications from this strike us as particularly important. One is that, if you do not need to know what the other person knows or thinks to improvise with them, then we can accept that beginners can interact musically with "experts." Understandings may be more consistent at some times than others, but this is not a prerequisite. This accounts for the ability of novices such as infants to participate in improvisation. They have not learnt how to understand their parents' vocal behaviour; they decide for themselves what to make of the sounds from the adults, respond however it strikes them to do so, and observe that in turn this generates more adult noises. If they like those noises, they will continue to take part, and trust becomes established, which can facilitate interaction.

The interaction of a music therapist and a client with no musical experience can be modelled in the same way, although this may raise some questions for how we understand music therapy to operate. Therapists expect to establish both trust *and* understanding of what their client means or feels or intends when they play (Gilboa, Bodner, and Amir 2006). The establishment of trust in a therapeutic relationship is undoubtedly important and a therapeutic component in what takes place. However, our findings suggest that even if they feel they have understood what is being played to them, any meanings ascribed to what the client plays can only ever represent a construction from the therapist's point of view, one that nevertheless opens up possibilities for therapeutic conversation (Wigram, 2004).

Another implication is that forming your own ideas about another person's tendencies, tastes, and abilities will shape your improvising without reproducing what they do. While it is perhaps not socially desirable to see oneself as influenced by the values or preferences of others, the findings suggest that it would be beneficial to encourage trainee improvisers to value what they bring to group improvisation themselves, whether or not they feel capable of what the others appear to know or do, and whether or not it represents accepted practice. The enjoyment of a very young child of their own voice in the soundscapes of adult talk is a useful model for prioritising one's own creative impulses. Furthermore, Bailey and others see improvisation as characterised by the quest for the new and unprecedented. If divergent understandings between improvisers' understanding can lead to startling new directions in their common improvisations, we might ask ourselves how such a "big-C" process of creativity can be defined and cultivated. Rather than a student judging their performance by whether it is likely to be understood and received as "correct" by other improvisers, they might develop stronger artistic identities and values through improvisation if they proceed through critical self-analysis of their own "tropes," or of how unusual their improvisations appear.

In the meantime, we can perhaps assert that trust and the choices two pianists make through a chance encounter around a street piano are sufficient for music to take place and to delight an audience, whether or not they have the same understanding of what they are doing.

6

A new virtuosity

Improvising over time

Improvisers who play together stay together. Pianist Aki Takase, commenting in an interview[1] on a recent duo recording with drummer Han Bennink, describes him as one of her "favourite drummers"; the two have interacted musically on many occasions over many years. In footage of the pair improvising on stage at Tampere Jazz festival in 2012,[2] Bennink drums in a way that an improviser who had not encountered him before might find extremely surprising or disorienting.

He first appears beating vigorously on the underside of a piano stool, before eventually returning to the drum kit. Takase begins to play abrupt, discordant descending figures interspersed with short jazz phrases, at which Bennink immediately drops his sticks a few times on the kit and flails at it with a cloth. As he starts to play with the sticks on the drums in short explosive flurries without a discernible pulse, the interaction takes on the character of call and response: as soon as one finishes, the other starts. The match between what each is playing is close, with descending pitches and jagged emphases strikingly replicated as the lead passes from one to the other. As Takase's choppy phrases gradually become more continuous, Bennink moves on to sustained patterns: a long rapid beat on closed hi-hat, rolls around the kit. Now playing together, they appear to arrive at the same perfectly synchronous accents within the stream of notes, and gradually the piece transforms into a march.

[1] "Thelonious Monk is the One," https://www.youtube.com/watch?v=ta-k7Iy_wRY
[2] https://www.youtube.com/watch?v=uKnYPqKvfVo

The Art of Becoming. Raymond A. R. MacDonald and Graeme B. Wilson, Oxford University Press (2020).

DOI: 10.1093/oso/9780190840914.001.0001

The apparent ease and nonchalance with which they navigate this short yet complex passage in synchrony is impressive. It is tempting to imagine that when they first played together, things might have been less fluent than this. Bennink's drum style is extremely and deliberately unconventional and startling, and Takase's approach to piano no less distinctive. Given the pair's history of playing together, their collaboration can be seen as a striking assimilation of each other's improvisational style. Given their smooth accommodation of surprising contributions from the other side of the stage we might presume that they have reached a stage where they know what the other will do and why. But if this were the case, why go to the effort of getting together to improvise again? Bennink has spoken of his persistent determination to innovate as a performer, and it seems reasonable to expect that this was the basis on which they decided to play as a duo one more time.

It is repeatedly emphasised in this book that improvisation is a universally accessible practice, that we are all improvisers. If so, why do we go to concerts to see someone in particular do this, or repeatedly listen to certain recordings of improvised music rather than others? Why go to the trouble and expense to hear someone do what we can do ourselves? Improvisers' practice is transformed the more they play. Their collaborative practice is also transformed the more they play with the same people, such that long-term improvising partners feel they are able to form *working predictions* of what each other might do. The reasons and processes behind such transformations are central to understanding how one can develop as an improviser or as an improvising group, and how improvising can best be taught as a creative practice.

This chapter considers

- how and why one might achieve or progress as an improviser;
- what one might strive for in individual and collaborative improvising;

- how improvisational development might be apprehended;
- how individuals can be supported in developing as improvisers; and
- how improvising is shaped by the ideas we can form about it, and the range of behaviours we can imagine.

We set out theoretical propositions to support the concept of development as an improviser. We also define capacities that might be associated with virtuosic improvising. We discuss the work of psychologist George Kelly, who argued that human beings are constantly testing and reshaping their individual understandings of the world, the better to predict social situations (Kelly, 2002). This theory offers a mechanism to explain how improvising relationships transform over time, and how improvisers can continue to exercise creativity together in real time.

How does an individual change their improvising?

Musicianship, as in other branches of the arts, is understood as a set of abilities that develop over time (Hargreaves and Lamont, 2017). This development can be facilitated and guided to particular ends through learning, teaching, and social processes (Figure 6.1), and to spectacular results in the case of stars whose performing commands mass audiences. What counts as virtuosic, however, varies from country to country, from continent to continent, and from one music scene to another. An uncanny facility with coaxing exotic soundscapes from a guitar amplifier may win plaudits in an experimental rock venue, yet leave audiences for gamelan music unimpressed. In a similar way, particular performers have come, over time, to improvise in individual and specialised ways that keep audiences around the world coming back to see them. An

Figure 6.1 Author RM improvising with school pupils at The Deeper Life School in Serrekunda, Gambia. Photo credit: Maya McCourt

improvised performance may be intriguing or astonishing if the performer achieves something through improvising that someone watching it could not achieve themselves.

The ability to perform like this may be something to aspire to, which invites the question of what it is about one person that makes their improvising so compelling. We have argued that particular knowledge or skills associated with a genre are not in themselves a measure of the broader capacity to improvise, and such badges of achievement are not necessarily meaningful to different audiences. Their appeal could instead lie in how they have learnt, over time, to navigate improvising: they are able to make choices and anticipate emerging situations in ways that are consistently surprising. People will carry on improvising or listening to improvising only if they continue to encounter something new or if they find that persevering leads to different outcomes; this is what sustains interest in any field.

For individuals to have the potential to become virtuoso improvisers in this sense, several propositions arise in relation to improvising:

1. *One can develop capacities as an improviser that are distinct from other aspects of musicianship.* The long hours a guitarist or bass player may spend jamming with friends are unlikely to be rewarding without a sense that something is being acquired that is different from just learning chord sequences or fingering patterns. They learn to interact in new ways with fellow musicians, to change what they are playing while playing with others, and to trust their ear and each other enough to try out something new halfway through. They are learning to achieve a sense of artistic collaboration. We discuss later in the chapter how these capacities might be defined.
2. *The attributes developed as an improviser are transferrable across genres or settings in ways that some other musical attributes are not.* If improvising is, like entrainment to a beat or rhythm, a universal that underpins music across human society and history, then development as an improviser should be applicable within different forms of music.
3. *All development as an improviser, whether infant, student, professional, or within a group, takes place along a common spectrum, and can therefore be supported and influenced.* If all development as an improviser is along a continuum, then perhaps we could do more to understand how this takes

place in every context, whether through apprenticeship with master musicians, in professional practice, within a community music group, or playing with friends after school. More importantly, it makes less sense to see community music as a separate thing from virtuosic professionalism; by following up a passion for improvising, the community musician is on a course towards virtuosity, whether they choose to take it that far or not.

4. *The directions and objectives for development across that spectrum are individually determined.* This fourth proposition raises many issues for evaluating or assessing improvisation, and for how it can best be taught and facilitated. In creative practice, any individual will work towards defining their own style and criteria. Self-expression is fundamental to the drive to improvise, and anything idiosyncratic is therefore valuable in improvisation. This is a central value in visual art education, yet it seems harder to accept that when someone strives to achieve virtuosity as a musical improviser, they might do so on their own terms.
5. *If we improvise in groups, development as an improviser is in the ability to collaborate in creative endeavour.* This last proposition highlights how important relationships are to growing as an improviser, in line with Vygotsky's understanding of the social mechanisms of development. Differences between improvisers shape relationships between them, in the same way that any individual differences determine who we form relationships with and how. In all areas of life, we interact with certain people most often, some people occasionally, and we avoid interaction with others. Improvisers form musical relationships over time with particular individuals; media interviews with someone who practices improvisation are likely to enquire about their regular collaborators. Improvisers tend to

affirm particular collaborations, to view certain long-term partnerships as involving a distinct category of practice, and to feel differently about improvising with people they know as compared to people they do not know (Wilson and MacDonald, 2017b). Here for example is a jazz trumpeter talking about who they play with:

> I've been doing gigs with the same people for a while, I think it certainly does, make the gig much more enjoyable. You get into it more, get to know each other's playing. (trumpeter quoted in MacDonald and Wilson, 2005)

As noted in chapter 5, Evan Parker has coined the term "tropes of practice" (Saunders, 2009) to refer to particular ways that he finds himself improvising with ensembles that have existed for many years: certain preferences or categories of response become recognisable from previous encounters and associated with what that group does. For instance, he states of one established ensemble:

> *sometimes with the trio with Barry and Paul we have to avoid too many slick endings, because if we want to we can finish on a six-pence kind of thing—"boom."* (quoted in Eyles, 2003)

Although others in the ensemble may perceive its tropes differently, such views underline that improvisers form particular expectations of certain individuals through repeated encounters, expectations that are influential upon their choices when improvising together. With a focus in literature on individual improvisers or occasions of improvisations, the processes behind this formation of improvising *relationships* are not clearly understood. In response to these propositions and the related issues outlined previously in this section, we propose a new conception of virtuosity.

A new virtuosity

The range or speed or physical control of sounds that one can execute; the understanding of existing music and how it has been produced; and facility with meta-techniques such as the reading of notation are all valuable in development as a musician towards particular ends. All of these fields of endeavour have an established pedagogy attached to them. The execution of a press roll on a snare drum, a close knowledge of the tradition of *lieder*, or rapid and accurate execution of the detailed musical instructions of a composer are recognisable objectives of musical practice. They can result in the achievement of key musical identities, or accolades and new capacities to delight and excite oneself, friends, and family or wider audiences. However, in contemporary practice, where musicians and other artists are increasingly valued for a spontaneous pick-and-mix approach to particular musical ends, and for the potential to execute unrehearsed musical feats, a separate strand of artistic development in improvising is important and rewarding as a field of endeavour that can integrate with many others in the gamut of genre practices. This strand of development is not clearly distinguished and theorised in current pedagogy for the arts.

A new virtuosity in improvisation might be defined in terms of

- confidence in exercising choice in real time;
- strength of personal rationale for such choices;
- sophistication and coherence of choices;
- discrimination and discernment of emerging performed material;
- facility in accommodating and responding to unprecedented or unexpected events; and
- integration and moderation of all the above within the context of a group.

All of these are dimensions on which we might wish to improve, or on which our development might impress others. Performers feel better if they are confident, and trusting one's own judgment is likely to lead to stronger artistic statements (Hickey, Ankney, Healy, and Gallo, 2016; Palmer, 2016). Sophistication is generally appreciated in any artistic endeavour, and the more differentiated we are able to make our improvisations, the richer one's potential performance. Improvisations also tend to impress more if they present a coherent, structured, or balanced whole, rather than appearing sporadic.

However, improvising is inescapably linked to artistic context. It requires the performer to take in and make sense of what is going on around them, and the more observant one is, the greater capacity one has to contribute artistically. In a performance where spontaneous novelty is the goal, the environment should ideally throw up surprises; and the better we are as improvisers, the more likely we are to embrace and use such events in creating live work. Finally, and crucially, an improviser's ensemble practice is more satisfactory the more they are able to tailor what they are doing to the overall objectives of a group. Thus, virtuosity as an improviser is essentially located within social interaction (Figure 6.2). Vocalist Maggie Nichols coined the term 'social virtuosity' to denote the capacity for effective interpersonal interaction that is acquired through, and essential for, successful improvisation in a group.

These qualities can all be mapped onto a developmental continuum, in the sense that any of us engaging in improvisation will exhibit them to varying extents on different occasions over time. Even in therapy, where improvisation takes place for clinical purposes, there is an anticipation of progression from session to session. If a client did exactly the same from one session to the next, they may be less engaged, and may not be seen to be making clinical progress. A virtuoso improviser, rather than occupying a special category of distinct performance practice, is someone who has persisted further than most in developing these same creative

Figure 6.2 Cross-disciplinary interaction in real time. Improvised music and dance at Something Smashing, Edinburgh. Left to right: Nicky Haire, Alma Lindenhovius, Russell Wimbish. Photo credit: Lucas Kao

faculties that an infant might use, to achieve particular and highly specialised aesthetic ends. What the qualities of the new virtuosity share is a focus on the prediction of situations encountered (artistic or social), and the choices that are consequently made. Psychological theories can help to conceptualise how improvisers develop to improvise in distinct ways through repeated encounters.

Theorising improvising relationships

Cannone and Aucouturier (2016) have argued that the more experience free improvisers have in playing this way (freely), the more closely they will share relevant mental models, or internal representations of how the music works (Gentner and Stevens,

1983). Their empirical evidence, based on how improvisers rate sound clips of others improvising, suggests that by repeatedly playing together, free improvisers acquire shared skills and knowledge that are particular to how they play together. They become in effect experts on what their particular group does. However, this model for development as an improviser raises again the issue of shared understanding: in a music where innovation is to be sought or expected, improvisers with the same ideas and understanding seem less likely to make surprising music together. It has been emphasised in previous chapters that musicians within an improvising ensemble can show divergent understandings of what they have been doing; and we have argued that if improvisation is to be creative, rather than simply reproducing styles, some degree of divergence in understanding may be essential.

The cognitive approach of Personal Construct Theory (PCT) (Kelly, 2002) holds that our psychological processes are channelled by how we anticipate events. Each person forms and transforms unique expectations to distinguish and predict what they encounter, based on their previous experience. These distinctions, or *personal constructs*, can be meaningfully applied to relevant people, things, or events (termed *elements*), to guide one's actions or responses, and are subject to change as an individual makes sense of successive situations. An individual might at first find someone *aloof* rather than *friendly*; after repeated encounters, they may adjust that evaluation, seeing them as more friendly, or see them in new terms altogether: say, *trustworthy* rather than *insincere*. Kelly thus viewed all human beings as scientists forming theories about any new person, thing, or situation in order to predict future encounters, then confirming or refining those theories as they go.

Two features of this theory in particular make it appropriate to understanding how improvisers interact and develop together. Since individual behaviour and decisions are rational only in terms of that person's own particular constructs, two people within a situation are not assumed to be judging it by the same criteria.

Also, an individual's personal constructs about someone else are understood to change through trial and error the more they are encountered, in order to make better predictions about what that other person does. They are only useful, and retained, if they allow someone to function in new situations.

PCT therefore suggests that an improviser adapting to a new collaboration, or to new circumstances within an existing collaboration, must develop constructs to function in that new role. As they successively negotiate improvising situations in a new collaboration, they may try out and acquire new ways of anticipating those situations that result in successful interaction with other improvisers. Another of Kelly's terms for PCT was "constructive alternativism," and these trials of new practice represent improvisers' constructive alternatives to what they might have done in previous improvisations. This process not only enables them to keep an ongoing collaboration fresh and rewarding, but also offers a means to keep up with a broader cultural scene that is constantly transforming itself.

PCT suggests that, rather than moving towards a shared understanding of improvising as they practice together, improvisers in a regular collaboration each progressively acquire more sophisticated yet idiosyncratic systems to differentiate what the group does. Each participant builds up over time constructs that help them to predict and make personal sense of what the others do. These sharpened expectations can shape and enhance their contributions in ways that the group will evaluate as successful, even if what they do is understood differently by each person or responded to in distinct ways. Patterns of choice may become apparent to each individual over repeated improvisations.

Someone who has improvised with another for a sustained period of time is, in Kelly's terms, someone who has developed sophisticated theories for that other person's improvisatory behaviour. Those theories are not necessarily "right" or shared by the other person, and are subject to change; but they help the improvisers to make confident contributions around each other. Those who keep coming back to improvise together are likely to have formed systems that are mutually satisfying.

Although a few studies have used PCT to examine how audiences discern jazz performances (Blowers and Bacon Shone, 1994; Holbrook and Huber, 1979, 1983) this approach has not previously been applied to creative improvisation (Winter and Reed, 2016). Yet PCT offers a potentially valuable means to measure, describe, and compare the flexible conceptual frameworks of very different artists. For instance, artists working in live (performative) drawing may see each improvised act within the context of a drawn object that remains present, while musicians may base their judgments on the memory of sounds over the course of the piece. To explore such issues further, one author (GW) convened a varied group of nine contemporary improvisers (three from each of the disciplines of music, dance, and visual art) using repertory grid methods (Fransella, Bell, and Bannister, 2004). All were recruited via a regular multidisciplinary improvisation night in one city, and therefore most knew of each other's practice to some extent.

The participants took part in short freely improvised performances bringing together either artists and dancers; dancers and musicians; or musicians and artists. The researcher analysed the video recordings to identify fifteen passages of around fifteen seconds that appeared to contain moments of change, five from each pair of disciplines. In subsequent individual interviews each participant watched and compare triads of events from their video, and described opposing qualities of those events in their own terms, a standard procedure for eliciting personal constructs in the PCT literature (Fransella et al., 2004). For instance, one musician distinguished events where he had perceived a "sense of the whole" from one where the group's actions appeared "random"; a dancer distinguished situations where she had acted on "impulse" from one where she had made a conscious "decision." Each interviewee then rated each of the ten events they had been involved in on each of their dimensions, on a scale from one (most like one label) to seven (most like the other label). The explanations they gave while answering were also recorded for analysis as qualitative data (see Table 6.1).

Table 6.1 shows the resulting grids of scores completed by three of the participants (dancer A, musician B, and artist B). These provide examples of the dimensions on which each performer evaluates their own improvised acts, and the improvised acts of others. Some considerations seemed to be similar across disciplines, for instance the conventional or otherwise nature of the improvising:

"quotidian" vs. "something mental" (musician B)
"within a form or mode" vs. "playful, unusual" (dancer A)

Or, consideration of whether one's contributions were consistent with those of other improvisers:

"same, complementary" vs. "different" (dancer A)
"following others in texture" vs. "trying to play differently from others" (musician B)
"following" vs. "going against" (artist B)

Although the semantic content of different individuals' constructs may appear related, the qualities are idiosyncratic in that they are always defined in the individual participant's terms. Other constructs appeared specific to individuals; for instance, only Dancer A was concerned with whether everyone was "upright" or "changing levels."

Some constructs held by improvisers from different disciplines may be equivalent in how they allow events to be distinguished while improvising. For instance, the five events involving musicians and dancers were rated with 87% similarity by dancer A on her construct *same, complementary* vs. *different*, and by musician B on his construct *clear what others are doing* vs. *no clear response*. Events

Table 6.1. Repertory grid data for three participants in the MISTI study (musician, dancer, and artist)*

	Construct label	MA2	MA8	MA10	MA13	MA14	MD3	MD5	MD6	MD9	MD11	AD1	AD4	AD7	AD12	AD15	Construct label
Musician	clear what others are doing	4	6	3	6	5	2	2	5	4	4						no clear response
	differently from others	1	1	1	3	2	2	5	3	2	2						following others in texture
	synchronised	6	7	2	6	6	2	3	6	1	3						different togetherness
	sense of the whole	4	2	3	7	5	3	3	6	2	6						random
	leading	2	3	2	3	6	2	6	5	6	4						listening/ responding
	something mental	4	2	3	4	3	4	4	6	5	3						quotidian
	what I'd imagine	1	4	2	6	5	2	4	6	2	3						different from what I'd imagine

	something recognisable	1	4	4	4	5	2	4	6	2	2						texture
	playing less	5	6	7	5	5	5	3	4	2	4						playing more
Dancer	do something						1	1	6	7	4	1	5	3	4	5	watching
	going in tempo						4	2	5	7	5	2	5	2	5	3	calibrating, change tempo
	same location						4	2	6	7	6	2	3	6	6	6	different location
	more level change						4	2	2	5	4	6	2	6	7	6	upright
	same/ complementary						4	2	4	5	4	2	6	6	5	2	different
	impulse						6	1	4	6	2	1	6	2	4	4	decision
	arrive at something						5	1	3	6	1	1	5	1	4	5	intervention

Continued

Table 6.1. Continued

	Construct label	MA2	MA8	MA10	MA13	MA14	MD3	MD5	MD6	MD9	MD11	AD1	AD4	AD7	AD12	AD15	Construct label
	physical contact						4	7	2	6	6	7	2	7	4	4	not touching
	connect to someone else						4	6	1	2	1	7	2	2	4	3	working independently
	playful, unusual						1	7	4	1	6	7	6	7	1	5	within a form. Mode
	duet/solo						4	2	7	7	7	1	1	2	6	1	trio
Artist	not sure what I'm doing	5	6	4	6	3						6	7	2	1	7	happens without thought
	punctuating space	1	1	6	1	1						4	5	4	1	4	filling space
	making beats	4	3	4	7	1						7	7	7	4	7	making lines
	following	1	4	1	5	7						1	1	3	5	2	going against
	reacting	1	4	3	2	1						1	1	3	1	2	in a bubble

watching	1	5	7	4	7	7	6	5	1	6	listening
thinking about drawers	1	4	5	4	7	7	7	6	7	6	thinking about the other discipline
small things	1	1	1	4	1	7	7	5	4	5	sweeping things
tuned in	2	4	5	1	2	1	2	4	7	1	anxious external factors
freer movements	7	5	6	3	7	1	1	2	7	1	restricted

* Columns correspond to video clips used as elements in the interviews; MA identifies clip from Musicians and Artists improvising together, etc. Participants only viewed and rated clips in which they had participated. Construct labels were suggested in pairs (left- and right-hand columns by each participant as opposing qualities of elements. Scores represent the participant's rating of each element on a scale of one to seven between the left-hand (1) and right-hand (7) labels.

that the dancer is likely to see as "complementary" are very likely to be seen by the musician as "clear," and so on. This offers as a basis for each to predict the other' reactions, even if they do not evaluate events in quite the same terms. These two dimensions can therefore be understood as functionally equivalent; despite being about different things, they allow different improvisers to distinguish emerging events in similar ways.

While the content of these distinctions, consistent with the idea of social construction, will vary considerably between individuals or between disciplines, the relationships between these constructs, and between constructs and elements, can be represented in spatial form using multivariate statistics. In this way a space can be mapped within which different events in the improvisation appear relatively close or distant—seen as more or less similar in terms of that person's own evaluative system. If elements appear grouped in similar ways by two improvisers, these individuals could be seen as likely to form similar understandings of those events, even if the meanings they attach to them, or the constructs they apply, are different.

Figures 6.3 and 6.4 were produced from a principal components analysis of the scores supplied by dancer A and musician B respectively, using Rep Plus v1.1 software (Gaines and Shaw, 2018). The two principal factors from each analysis are plotted as the x- and y-axes in the respective charts for each participant. The two figures suggest that these two improvisers made different sense of what was going on while improvising together, in that the events are grouped quite distinctly in the two spaces in the figures. For the dancer, for example, events MD3 and MD11 are at opposite extremes, and therefore seen as very different; while for musician A, MD3 and MD11 are in the same quadrant, occupying a similar conceptual space. This approach suggests that the content of the improvisers' constructs and the relationships between them can in this way be mapped onto the

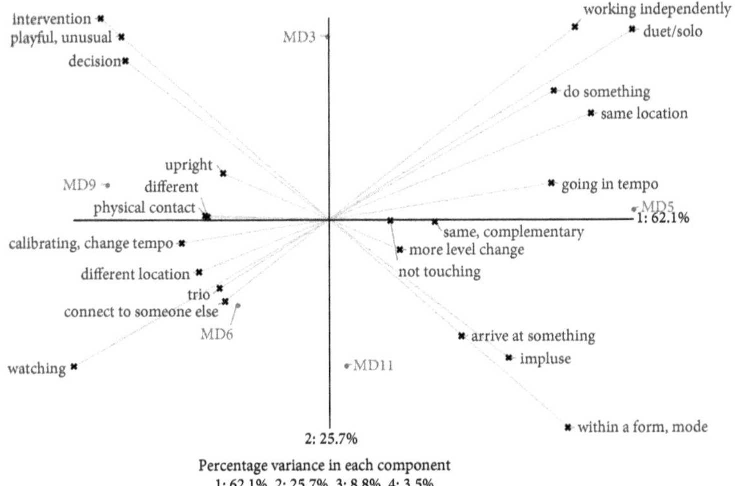

Figure 6.3 Principal components analysis of repertory grid data from dancer A

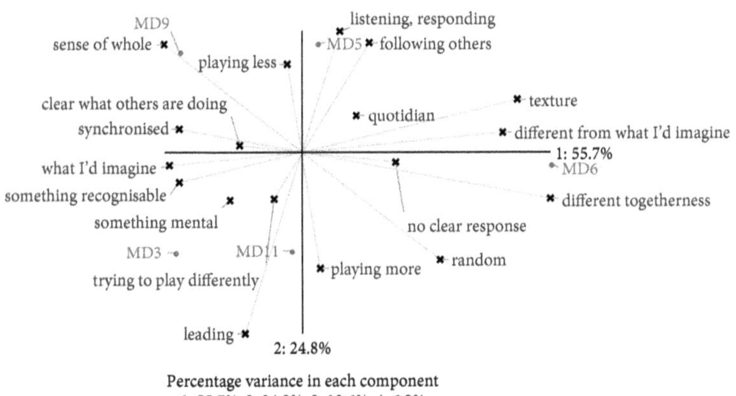

Figure 6.4 Principal components analysis of repertory grid data from musician B

elements of the new virtuosity described earlier, leading to the following assertions:

- Developing a richer set of personal constructs and finding that these allow one to predict improvising situations to one's satisfaction is likely to give confidence in exercising artistic choice in real time.
- Constructs are understood to be personally meaningful rather than objectively defined; the more one is aware of and able to access such personal rationales, the stronger one's capacity for choice will be.
- Having more ways to make increasingly fine-grained distinctions between improvising situations equates to the capacity for sophisticated and coherent choice.
- If an improviser can understand different performed events in such a way that they are dispersed across the conceptual space of their construct system, rather than all being seen as similar and occupying the same space, then they have greater capacity to discriminate and discern patterns that emerge in improvised performance.
- The flexibility and adaptability that construct systems are understood to possess offer a model of the capacity to accommodate and respond to unprecedented or unexpected events. Rather than the rigid concept of a skill set or body of knowledge, the notion of a set of personal propositions that are continually tested and revised to cope with new situations is an excellent way to understand virtuosic improvisers' capacity to embrace and pursue spontaneous innovation in their creative practice.
- Construction is a social process; the theory outlined by Kelly seeks to explain how human beings interact, learn from each other, and arrive at mutually satisfying behaviour. In this sense a developed and well-functioning system of constructs for improvising will facilitate the integration and moderation of other virtuosic capacities within the context of a group.

Conclusions and implications

In this chapter

- We have identified key implications of the idea of a virtuoso improviser.
- On the basis of those propositions, we have set out six key acquirable and measurable qualities that can define virtuosity as an improviser.
- We have shown that personal construct theory offers a valuable basis on which to explain how these qualities might be developed.
- We have demonstrated how PCT methods can be used to assess the nature and application of those qualities in improvisers from different disciplines.

The arguments, methods, and evidence in this chapter offer a powerful resource for facilitating the development of improvisers towards virtuosity through education and community music.

The interview responses underline that improvisers do not have to share understanding of what each other is doing in order to improvise together (Wilson and MacDonald, 2017a). Indeed, individuals whose practice is primarily in one field of music, dance, or visual art might be expected to lack expertise and knowledge in each other's fields. Yet they can, and do, spontaneously create improvised performances. This indicates that whatever sense they are able to make lets them respond in ways that map onto actions from other disciplines.

PCT techniques provide an invaluable way to consider the relationships between improvisers without assuming they share an understanding of what they are doing. Two members of an ensemble may not think exactly the same way about what the group is doing but still arrive at expectations that allow them to perform in a consistent manner, or that allow others who know them to respond readily. The idea of a system of constructs specific to improvising is an effective means to conceptualise the five propositions at the start of this chapter.

The specific attributes one develops as an improviser can be understood as a series of personally meaningful dimensions on which to evaluate and predict a broad range of improvising situations. These constructs are distinct from other aspects of performance in which one might develop, in that they allow one to make a spontaneous creative response within live performing situations. They may only be relevant to situations where two or more people improvise together; they may not allow one to act out, say, the ballet role of Coppelia, where other constructs are applicable. But without being able to evaluate and attach meanings to what is going on in the environment of a live improvisation, one cannot begin to take part in it.

In largely *non*-improvised music, where written notes have to be executed at the right time in an accepted way, there is much less scope for choice for the performer, and therefore less opportunity to deploy constructive alternatives. It is more consequential in an opera if performance expectations are not validated, since the details of the music are supposed to be substantially recognisable. Someone learning to sing opera will have to develop very specific systems of constructs in order to respond effectively when performing a score; for instance, different ways of representing vowel sounds that are not transferable to other genres. Even in improvised genres, constructs such as *swing* vs. *straight* or *Bill Evans* vs. *Red Garland voicings* on the piano are specific to the genre of jazz. However, constructs such as "connect to someone else" vs. "working independently" are broad enough to apply to many creative contexts, and would provide the improviser with a means to try interacting with any form of performance. One can therefore acquire and refine constructs as an improviser that are transferrable across genres, scenes, and disciplines in ways that some other musical ways of thinking are not.

A construct system is a flexible and adaptive structure, and therefore any development as an improviser can take place across a continuum that is always amenable to developmental support or influence. Ideas one has as an infant about different sounds, movements, or images (say, *happy* vs. *sad* or *funny* vs. *serious*); as a novice instrumentalist (say, *major* vs. *minor*); or as a professional musician encountering new practices for the first time (say, *wistful* vs. *exuberant*) may all be progressively augmented and refined to distinguish aesthetic settings that earlier constructs do not sufficiently predict (e.g., movements that are angry or suggest animals, or music in no readily discernible key). Although the proliferation of constructs, and their expansion into different systems convenient to different performance contexts, allows increasingly fine-grained expectations to be formed, the early constructs can continue to be applied for the rest of one's life: music or dance may always be happy or sad, whatever other distinctions one can make about it. Finally, the "personal" in PCT is entirely consistent with the idea that each improviser's constructs for improvising will not correspond exactly to those of anyone else. Each person's unique trajectory of aesthetic, social, and cultural experiences ensures that in creative practice, they will follow bespoke directions as long as they are allowed to determine their own creative output.

But compatible responses can still be arrived at by two people with their different systems. For example, one member of a group might be focused on the sadness of a moment, while another on the slowness of what is taking place. Either may still choose to play a long low note or find it appropriate for the other to do this, even though their reasons for choosing or endorsing this are different. Judgments of the appropriateness (musical or social) of an individual's ideas and responses are socially or culturally determined, rather than objectively measurable. They may be a concern for teachers working to a curriculum or to personal development goals for their students. However, judgments of aesthetic value are entirely personal.

Behaviour as improvisers is fundamentally shaped by the ideas we can form about improvising situations, but is also limited by the range of improvised responses we can imagine and execute. In the process of learning to discern and evaluate musical situations, one also acquires an expanding repository of possible musical responses to those situations. These may include musical practices or techniques associated with specific genres, but if we understand the decision to apply them as entirely driven by personal constructs rather than by genre requirements, we realise that they may be brought to bear in any situation. A tabla player improvising with rock musicians is still likely to play mostly material they have learned through the tabla repertoire; if that is where they have spent most time developing as a musician, that repertoire represents most of what they are likely to do in response to other improvisers.

Our use of PCT technique to date has been limited to consideration of a single session for improvising by individuals relatively new to each other's practice. However, a study gathering constructs and ratings around group improvisations from the same people at regular intervals over time might indicate whether the organisation of events and evaluative dimensions in improvisers' conceptual space can change over time or acquire similarity in *structure* if not in *semantic content*; and whether the discrimination one can bring to bear on someone else's improvising develops or expands through repeated creative interaction. Even if two improvisers' approach is not informed by the same body of knowledge and skills, they may through repeated playing together arrive at ways of improvising that are increasingly compatible.

That, after all, is why we spend time improvising and why improvising with others sustains our interest and excitement over a lifetime. The more time an individual spends in this pursuit, the more alternatives they find they can perceive and execute in spontaneous interaction. But the more time they spend doing so with the same collaborators, the more elaborate are the ideas that they can form about how those particular people will improvise; and the greater the range of expectations and responses they will be able to form, try out, and have confirmed or refuted. That is not to say that the individual would have learned by that time how they would play in any given situation—in which case it might have become boring to play with them. Instead, the individual would have been developing their own ways to anticipate what someone else might do, to expand the range of what was possible with them. The idea of a capacity for improvising that can be developed and is applicable to any collaboration lets us think in new ways about how to teach improvisation, or to progress with it in personally satisfying ways.

In this chapter we have proposed a specific set of capacities that can be developed or heightened through improvising over an extended period of time. We suggest these are relevant to any art form or type of improvised interaction. We have argued that building and refining these capacities constitutes development towards a new virtuosity. We have also proposed that personal construct theory offers a valuable means to understand how this development takes place, and how these skills are applied across genre or disciplinary boundaries. These insights offer a new framework for the teaching of improvisers, supporting them to achieve the close interaction of performers such as Bennink and Takase.

7

Improvisation and health

Why improvising is good for you

"Music begins where the possibilities of language end" (Sibelius, 1919). This well-known Jean Sibelius quote points to the ambiguous, yet deeply personal and unconscious aspects of musical communication. It is these features, combined with its ability to profoundly engage psychologically and culturally, that make music a unique channel of communication. These features are also at the heart of why music can be a catalyst for positive personal change. There are many ways in which music can be used for therapeutic purposes. For example, music listening can reduce pain (Mitchell and MacDonald, 2012) and ameliorate the impacts of dementia (MacDonald and Wilson, 2014). Musical participation can enhance communication skills for individuals with learning difficulties (MacDonald and Miell, 2002) or enhance coping strategies for individuals with mental health problems (McFerran, 2012).

This chapter focuses specifically upon the use of musical improvisation for health and well-being. We consider the fundamental features of improvisation and link them specifically to possible health and well-being improvements. A model showing the different types of communication processes involved is also presented.

Chapter 2 highlighted improvisation as an accessible, social, creative, and non-verbal process, distinct from other areas of musical activity. It is these features that make it well suited to health and well-being applications. There are many anecdotal examples of improvisation being used to enhance or maintain health. American pianist Keith Jarrett's reputation as one of the most influential

The Art of Becoming. Raymond A. R. MacDonald and Graeme B. Wilson, Oxford University Press (2020).

DOI: 10.1093/oso/9780190840914.001.0001

contemporary jazz musicians is partly built upon his approach to improvisation. In 1996 he was diagnosed with chronic fatigue syndrome and stopped all public performances. He used music as a means of coping with illness and also used his illness as a way of inspiring new music, stating that the illness was "a great educator." He famously recorded "The Melody of the Night, With You," not only as a Christmas gift to his wife, but also as a way of aiding recovery out of chronic fatigue syndrome. The Inner Revolution Society, based in Los Angeles, USA, uses improvisation as a technique to help woman and teenage girls recover from addiction.[1] Their workshop programmes are targeted at developing group work, trust, and listening. Using theatre-based activities the sessions aim to develop self-confidence, improve self-esteem, and reduce anxiety through improvisation.

While these two examples are very different, they share two key points: improvisation is the primary activity and there are links between the improvisation activities and health and well-being outputs. Improvisation has long been associated with the potential to bring about improvement in health. Indeed, it is a key process used by music therapists, and early texts outlining music therapy practice contained numerous examples of improvisational activities (Alvin, 1978; Nordoff and Robbins, 1965). This chapter draws these processes and potential outcomes together and explains four characteristics of musical improvisation identified as underpinning the health benefits:

- Improvisation links conscious with unconscious processes.
- Improvisation makes unique demands on cognition.
- Improvisation facilitates creative interaction.
- Improvisation enables the non-verbal expression of thoughts and feelings that may otherwise be difficult to express.

[1] http://innerrevolutionsociety.com

Before we address these mechanisms, we discuss some fundamental features of improvisation important within health and well-being contexts.

Improvisation as social process

Musical improvisation provides a unique social context and has potential for developing a host of skills that relate to health and well-being. For example, group improvisation involves sophisticated social and musical negotiation. Musical choices (as discussed in chapter 4) about when to play, when to stop, how loudly to play, when to support another member of the group with quiet material, when to introduce new material, etc. are all key decisions for an improviser. These decisions are undertaken regardless of the skill level or experience. Therefore, a five-year old child or a world-class trumpeter must make exactly the same type of decisions (albeit with different material) when engaged in group improvisation. These decisions are musical and social. In many ways they echo decisions made in daily life: when to enter a conversation, when to listen, when to develop a new point, extend one that has ready been made, etc. Functioning effectively in group situations is a key part of daily life involving complex and spontaneous decision making. Reading non-verbal cues, anticipating consequences of actions, developing empathy, and interpersonal understanding are ubiquitous everyday social tasks.

The type of skills required to work in group music improvisation contexts may be transferable to social situations given the spontaneous, social, creative, and universally accessible nature of improvisation. This makes improvisation a situation where individuals of all ages, experiences, and backgrounds can develop important social as well as musical skills. Improvisation involves real time decision making, risk taking, and complex collaborative negotiation strategies. It is therefore a particularly sophisticated type of socially mediated artistic collaborative endeavour. This way of conceptualising improvisation emphasises psychological and group processes rather than acoustic parameters and musical structures. Rather than viewing improvisation as a rarefied form of musical communication, open to the initiated few who have developed advanced technical skills and musical knowledge, improvisation can be conceptualised as mapping directly onto daily life. Thus, when improvising we deploy strategies used for negotiating life. Taking this view of improvisation allows links to be made between musical improvising and other types of social interactions. In the appropriate contexts (e.g., with a music therapist), improvising musically with others may help individuals gain new insight into relating to other people. Improvisation can thus be viewed as an important musical technique used to facilitate psychological developments.

Improvisation and music therapy

The most detailed accounts of health and well-being effects of improvising come from music therapy literature (MacDonald and Wilson, 2014; Sutton, 2002). In music therapy, improvisation is viewed as a vital musical technique used to help establish and maintain therapeutic relationships (Rolvsjord, Gold, and Stige, 2005). There are a considerable number of different approaches to employing improvisation within therapeutic frameworks (Stensæth, 2017). Improvisation is key to Creative Music Therapy founded by Paul Nordoff and Clive Robbins and to Psychodynamic approaches (Trondalen and Bonde, 2012). One important feature of the Nordoff-Robbins approach is that therapists work in pairs, one typically playing piano (sometimes guitar) supporting client's improvisations and the other directly facilitating the client's developing improvisations (Nordoff and Robbins, 1965).

Improvisation is used extensively in psychodynamic approaches to music therapy. The psychodynamic approach contends that when we speak, move, think, interact, and generally exist, there are deep and influential emotions, urges, and feelings beyond conscious awareness. These features may motivate actions and be expressed symbolically in behaviours (Levy and Ablon, 2009). Music is an excellent vehicle for this type of unconscious expression of personality features. A key aspect of a psychodynamic approach emphasises the link between the musical improvisations and talking about improvisation. For example, following an improvisation, a therapist may discuss the client's musical choices made and will negotiate an interpretation of the improvisation that relates to important issues. Utilising a psychodynamic interpretation, the beat of a drum is not only a rhythmic pulse but it could also be an unconscious expression of an emotion (e.g., anger or love) of which the performer may not be immediately aware. The origins of this emotion or feeling may date from years earlier, the precise detail of which may reside within the unconscious. Priestley (1985) was one of the first music therapists to write about how psychodynamic aspects of daily life could be explored in therapeutic sessions. Here clients would discuss key concerns and then be invited to explore them musically during a session. The music produced and client's resultant feelings would be discussed after the session (Brescia, 2004).

Improvising in therapeutic contexts offers specific benefits to particular populations, including the amelioration of neurological damage, improvements in mental health conditions, reductions in stress and anxiety, and improved communication and joint attention behaviours in children with autism spectrum disorders, and also patients in a cancer hospice. MacDonald and Wilson (2014) provide a detailed overview of the different types of populations and outcomes reported in these and other studies. Erkkilä et al. (2011) investigated how specific psychodynamic processes such as self-projection and free association within improvisation can facilitate an exploration of important memories and issues. This team also investigated the effects of improvisational music therapy on the treatment of depression and developed detailed systematic protocols for this type of work (Erkkilä et al., 2008). Fachner, Gold, and Erkkila (2013) highlight the effects of improvisation upon brain function in individuals with depression. These authors show how improvisation during music therapy affects cortical activity in the frontotemporal regions of the brain, suggesting anxiety reduction.

With Improvisation being an important part of music therapy practice, music therapists' training places importance upon understanding the process and outcomes of improvisational activities (Trondalen and Bonde, 2012). Wigram (2004) delineates some key principles and techniques associated with improvisation in music therapy. He outlines the types of improvisation therapists can use by describing and categorising specific musical strategies. In

Figure 7.1 Music therapists Nicky Haire, Becky White, and Philippa Derrington improvising with dance therapists Helga Margrét Schram, Vicky Karkou, and Suzi Cunningham at Concurrent #2, Edinburgh, 2017. Photo credit: Full Zoom Photography

Mirroring the therapist imitates or copies what the client is playing and in doing so offers clear signals that the therapist is listening and responding to client's music phrases. With *Matching* the therapist provides improvised material that is similar but not identical to what clients is playing. *Empathic improvising and reflection* involves the therapist playing improvised music with the client that aims to provide support and emotional confirmation. The therapist helps to create a turn taking type of improvisation similar to conversation when using *Dialoguing* approaches. A constant repetitive rhythm or tonality is created in *Stabilising techniques* while *Modelling* provides improvised material for the client to respond to or develop. These techniques highlight specific ways in which therapists use different types of improvisatory approaches for enhancing musical interactions and developing the ongoing therapeutic relationship in clinical settings.

The previous paragraphs have highlighted some important features related to how music therapists use improvisation, however one important question is: *what are the features of improvisation activities that produce these beneficial effects?* In this next section we turn our attention to this question by highlighting the four features mentioned at the start of the chapter: links to unconscious; unique demands on cognition; emotional engagement and creative interaction.

Key features of improvising that influence health

Improvisation links conscious with unconscious processes

The unconscious is composed of internal psychological processes of which we are unaware. It includes automatic behaviours (breathing, walking), events, and feelings that while we have no immediate access to understand, still influence our actions on a moment-to-moment basis. The spontaneous real-time nature of improvisation facilitates an immediate connection with unconscious processing. Improvisation places significant cognitive demands upon us while at the same time necessitating real-time, in-the-moment decision making. This makes the possibility of unconscious expression more likely. Accessing unconscious processes during or after an improvisation can be helpful in therapeutic terms because our daily interactions are influenced by unconscious processes. Problematic patterns of behaviour and interaction may have unconscious influences. Bringing these influences into conscious awareness may help an individual understand the problem and perhaps adapt more "healthy" ways of relating and thinking (Borden, 2009).

Improvisation makes unique demands on cognition

We have demonstrated throughout this book that psychological decisions need to be made when improvising. This makes improvising cognitively engaging, and it may also provide a context that facilitates a psychological move away from preoccupying negative thoughts and feelings. Improvisation may therefore produce distraction from negative type of thinking and automatic thoughts that may be dysfunctional and causing anxiety, stress, or other types of psychological turbulence. This ability of improvisational activities to facilitate a type of distraction is a further reason why it may be beneficial for health.

Improvisation facilitates creative interaction

Improvisation, as a unique form of creative, collaborative group communication, promotes interaction and social engagement. Figure 7.1 shows music therapists, drama therapists, musicians and dancers collaborating using improvisation as the primary creative process. Creative interaction is a fundamentally important part of the improvisational process and one possible reason why improvisation can have positive effects on health and well-being.

Being socially engaged within a safe and therapeutic environment can have significant positive effects on important psychological aspects of personality such as "agency." Having a robust sense of agency has long been held as an important psychological feature of a healthy, well-adjusted contemporary life. Agency refers to a subjective sense of being an individual and in control of one's own actions, thoughts, and feelings (Jeannerod, 2003). To some extent we are not aware of our own sense of agency since it refers to a sense of control over thoughts and actions that exists at the preconscious level. It also refers to the ability to be flexible, stable, and resilient, and crucially influences our understanding of ourselves as a separate person. Improvisation may have significant benefits for our sense of agency as it offers opportunities for creative engagement in important and significant ways. Pouthlaki et al. (2008) highlighted the positive effects of an improvisation music therapy programme for individuals in a cancer hospice. These individuals had no previous experience of music making and so engaging in improvisation may have helped promote a sense of agency via opening up new avenues to creativity. Also, since participants were playing improvised music, they were playing their own music, not someone else's. These experiences may result in an increased sense of agency and this increased sense of agency may have resultant positive effects upon health and well-being. The following example is from a participant in a group improvisation session for individuals at a cancer hospice.

> And then if you hear someone, you can pick up their rhythm and you can join in as well or maybe pick up someone else and join in with them. So, everybody is playing a tune and everybody is communicating and you can pick, you know, certain tunes or

> sounds or rhythms if you like and join in with the other person. (Pothoulaki et al., 2008)

This highlights how someone with no previous music experience can engage musically and communicate meaningfully in a group situation. This expressed sense of meaningful engagement is directly linked to a sense of agency and is implicated in general improvements in health and well-being. Also, the group situation creates a type of musical and psychological gestalt, where the individual components of the socio-music experience is greater than the sum of the parts. For example, beating a simple rhythm on a large drum may sound and feel superficial and meaningless when carried out alone. However, when undertaken as part of a collective endeavour it can provide an important input for the whole group, acting as a musical anchor or a solid home point for the rest of the participants. It can be a point of sharing, and it can connect where other members of group also join with this rhythm. This rhythm can thus be an important communicative device within the creative music group context. Importantly, it can have negative consequences as well. Perhaps the constant repetition may engender a sense of coercion where other members of the group feel they must also join with the tempo. Thus, it is important that therapists are alert to possible subtle shifts in meaning or the multiplicity of meanings that can occur during group improvisation sessions. Exploring our feelings through communicating improvisatorily with someone else allows us to develop alternative identities which can also be therapeutic in a number of ways. As discussed in chapter 4 decision making is a crucial aspect of improvisation and implicated with the creative interactional component of improvisation. One has agency in shaping self and music, and improvisation facilitates this type activity. Therefore, improvisation can develop agency in the sense that we can develop new identities through improvisation activities. Improvisation also produces neurological engagement and recent advances in brain imagining techniques have produced compelling evidence demonstrating that a brain that engages with music is changed by music (Thault, 2010).

Improvisation enables the non-verbal expression of troublesome emotions

Improvisation provides the possibility for spontaneous, real-time, and immediate emotional connection through music. Participants can express deep emotions without necessarily being able to verbalise them. In some cases, they will not be aware of these emotions while playing. A therapist may be able to bring these emotional features into conscious awareness at a later point by discussing possible meanings and significance. Resultantly, an immediate and direct connection with emotional engagement is a primary reason why improvisation can have health benefits. The creative engagement therefore provides a means of exploring important issues in a different way from language. This environment may be safer and less intimidating than a spoken conversation since the dialogue is abstract.

Expressing thoughts and feelings in music that are important but unable to be articulated verbally can be beneficial in helping tackle complex and difficult life situations. Why is this the case? On the one hand the inability to express important issues may produce negative thoughts and emotions such as anxiety and stress. When improvising, people may be able to communicate these feelings non-verbally via music. The expression of these feelings can produce a type of emotional release sometimes termed catharsis and this can have a positive effect upon health and well-being.

Engaging in improvisation is also an embodied activity. Embodiment emphasises the role that the physical body has in shaping how we think and act. In particular, musical embodiment emphasises how the body is used in musical performance.

For example, beating a drum, strumming a guitar, and shaping our vocal chords all involve advanced motor coordination (Lesaffre, Maes, and Leman, 2017). Therefore, all music is embodied, and all improvisation is embodied. Viewing improvisation as a type of embodied communication highlights the physicality as well as the spontaneity of music. The embodied nature of improvisation—the spontaneous ways in which bodies must move and co-ordinate to communicate musical ideas—necessitates advanced and sometimes intuitive movements. This type of coordinated activity that lies at the heart of improvisation can have positive effects for heath and well-being, producing a significant and tangible connection between thoughts, emotions, and specific body movements. This can motivate further musical engagement and is a crucial factor in understanding how we communicate spontaneously together.

A model for improvisation health and well-being

The previous paragraphs have outlined *why* improvisation can be useful for health-related applications of music. Perhaps the next obvious questions is *how* improvisation functions in these contexts. In the following section we present a model for understanding how improvisation operates within music to affect health (MacDonald and Wilson, 2014).

The flow chart shown in Figure 7.2 summarises the ways in which improvisation can affect health and well-being. Not just in therapy but also in other settings such as education or general music making. It makes a distinction between improvised elements and non-improvised elements in music making. The improvised elements afford particular types of opportunity for beneficial effects upon health and well-being. In the preceding paragraphs, we identified four key processes that may produce positive effects and have incorporated them into the model. We

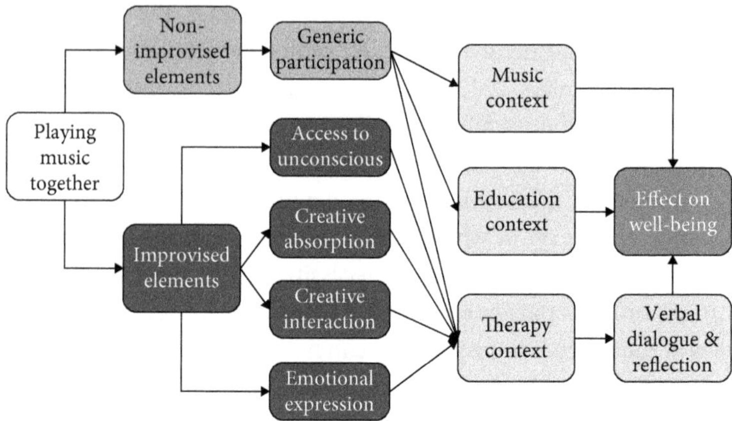

Figure 7.2 Flow chart for the effects of musical improvising on health and well-being

suggest that any or all of these elements can be present to varying degrees within improvised music. Since these elements may be presented to differing degrees in different interventions and for different people, we have represented them as having separate lines of influence within the model. For, example one individual may experience a cathartic unconscious revelatory moment during an intervention. Meanwhile another may find the creative challenge of maintaining an interaction with a guitarist as a particularly rewarding musical encounter during the same musical interactions. If these events occur in a therapy context, then the therapist may choose to discuss these events and their significance with the client. However, these types of experience can also occur in performance contexts where the focus is upon delivering a musical output for an audience Also of vital importance in the model are the different contexts in which the improvisatory encounters occur, namely, educational, therapeutic, and musical contexts since the objectives, processes, and outcomes may be distinctive for each context.

Engaging in an improvisation with a therapist in a hospital will be very different from improvising in a weekly community drum circle. These two situations will be different from a free improvisation concert with bass and cello in a bar. Yet they will all contain some similar elements as suggested by the model described in the preceding sections (unconscious processes, creative engagement, creative absorption, and emotional expression) and may lead to possible beneficial outcomes for the participants. Of course, every improvisatory context is unique, and this model is an attempt to draw together some overarching similarities between all types of improvisation and summarise the possible ways in which improvisation functions in health-related situations. Also, there may be overlap between the different contexts. A community-based music therapy intervention focused on improvisational drumming may share some similar features with a weekly drum circle meeting in a school hall. They may both share a focus upon emphasising that mistakes are unimportant as all types of musical participation and expression are equally valued, the emphasis being upon a participatory approach to musical engagement. This also has implications for how improvisation is undertaken in these different situations as a therapist may wish to examine the improvisational practices of a community music group in a different way from a teacher or community musician. However, the parallels and contrasts between community music education and broader performance, and the intersection of therapeutic, educational, and social objectives, are exciting areas for future research.

It is also important to point out that improvisation as a process is neither good nor bad, but rather it is how people engage with improvisation that may produce beneficial effects. It could also be possible to produce deleterious effects where negative thinking and mental health problems can be exacerbated. For example, improvisation may reinforce automatic negative thinking. This is a type of recurrent thought involving free floating negative cognitions that can influence an individual's views across many situations. It is linked to depression and a general negative outlook (Oldham, Skodol, and Bender, 2014). Those engaged with improvisation for health and well-being objectives should be aware that improvisation may facilitate these types of thoughts.

Wordless, improvised music can be interpreted in myriad ways and this ambiguity of meaning is one of the primary reasons why it feels easier to associate emotions with spontaneous music. However, this makes drawing emphatic and clear meanings difficult. While improvisation provides a direct link to the unconscious, the way in which the unconscious is made manifest becomes complex. Ascribing meaning to improvisations presents a particular challenge for therapists, or indeed anybody, to confidently unravel from music interactions. However, therapists are acutely aware of this dilemma and are able to build multiple meanings into verbal analysis of improvisations. Therapists are trained to listen to many different elements in the music and also pay particular attention to other gestures (Skewes-McFerran and Wigram, 2002).

Listeners interpret the meaning of improvised music within a constantly evolving stream of influences such as culture, personality, expectations, previous experience, etc. This allows for personal associations to emerge in the music. This type of ambiguity is celebrated across art forms and creative practices where meaning is constructed along an infinite number of dimensions. However, within healthcare research epistemologies one goal is to reduce ambiguity by accurately predicting the effects of specific interventions like music therapy. This is important because healthcare goals are to enhance well-being, alleviate suffering, and ameliorate pain and distress. With time and resources in demand like never before, researchers working in this area seek to reduce ambiguity to further knowledge about how interventions can be developed and delivered. Therefore, in attempting to contribute to the growing body of knowledge investigating the health benefits of improvisation, this chapter (and this book) is both a celebration of, and desire to reduce, ambiguity.

Conclusion

Music is not a universal language; it is a unique channel of interaction which offers communicative possibilities quite different from any other medium. While many authors have conceptualised music as being the same as, or very similar to, language, it is a cliché to think of music as such. However, its communicative properties mean it can have a significant role to play in health and well-being applications of music. This chapter has highlighted how key features of improvisation can facilitate improvements in health and well-being, and we have shown how these components can combine within a model of improvisation.

While there is a growing body of research highlighting the use of improvisation for positive psychological outcomes, there is still a need to understand more precisely the processes and outcomes of these interventions in contemporary contexts. Future research should also consider how improvisation may also have preventive effects. For example, engaging in improvisation may slow down cognitive and physical deterioration associated with Alzheimer's or Parkinson's disease or alleviate symptoms of depression as well as other conditions (Erkkilä, 2009). Future research could also investigate this issue in both clinical and non-clinical contexts including music therapy, community, and educational settings. Mixed-methods approaches using both quantitative and qualitative techniques could offer holistic accounts of the lived experienced of improvisation (MacDonald and Wilson, 2014). When improvisation is viewed as a sophisticated form of social interaction, links to other non-musical contexts and the implications for health and well-being are clear.

8
The way forward

Over the previous eight chapters we have explored various ways in which improvisation is an important social creative and collaborative process. In this final chapter we present summaries of our key issues, offering some overarching themes that tie these concepts together and point the way forward for future research.

New vistas of practice

Chapter 1 highlighted that improvisation has moved to the heart of contemporary arts practice and programming. It is now a central way of developing new work and fostering collaboration, with festivals and venues around the world regularly programming artists for whom improvisation will be a significant part of their practice and artistic identity. Improvisation can foster new ways of thinking and working artistically and will continue to develop as a field of practice aligned with social, cultural, and technological developments. Improvisers constantly attempt to innovate and progress their work to develop new principles of practice and to distinguish their own approaches from those of others. In the future we expect to see more merging of genres and cross-disciplinary engagement through improvisation, and more applications in other fields, and the expansion of improvisatory practice through new technologies. The growth of improvisation will also extend to forging new links between disciplines and practitioners.

There are many contemporary practitioners reshaping existing genres through improvisation. For instance, folk traditions are

The Art of Becoming. Raymond A. R. MacDonald and Graeme B. Wilson, Oxford University Press (2020).

DOI: 10.1093/oso/9780190840914.001.0001

fostering outstanding performers with authoritative command of those genres whose practice is increasingly shaped by their embrace of post-genre improvising. Italian saxophonist Christian Ferlaino whose in-depth study of the structure and devices of Calabrian Italian folk music have shaped a radical praxis in composition and solo saxophone improvising (Ferlaino, 2018). Improvisers within the Scottish scene, such as the trio Lau[1] or clarsach player Catriona Mackay,[2] combine working from within the Scottish folk music tradition, experimenting with cutting edge technology, and collaborating internationally. Festivals dedicated to cultural exchange through improvisation are important initiatives in developing such practice. There is a need to document this emergent scene as such, and to write or theorise about what characteristics are shared in their diverse approaches, and how their work is informed by the different character and practices associated with their respective traditions.

Throughout this book we have discussed examples of improvisers from different disciplines coming together in performance. This is still a relatively haphazard field driven by the personal projects and interests of different individuals, and one which can be difficult to present to funding bodies or promoters if expectations are informed by only one discipline. The existence of this underground DIY scene is crucial to the development of improvised music as it gives access to public performance and opportunities for artists who may not get the opportunities to perform at more established venues and festivals. Improvisation offers a means not only to hurdle disciplinary boundaries but also to begin to remove them. Importantly, we view improvisation as a discrete field of practice in which live painters, dancers, spoken word artists, and musicians can locate their work. Thus, they can feel themselves to be among a far larger pool of like-minded practitioners.

[1] http://www.lau-music.co.uk
[2] http://www.catrionamckay.co.uk

This post-genre approach will foster new ideas, taking improvisation, the art of becoming, the art of the unrepeatable, into new areas of practice. For instance, The Great Barrier Orchestra is a cross-disciplinary project developed by Swedish sound artist Ann Rosen.[3] It incorporates visual art, music, and performance utilising newly developed electronic instruments with a particular focus on how choices and decisions are made during the artistic process. In one performance, an artist draws with charcoal on a sheet of paper while computer software translates the drawing into sound. The drawing is projected on a screen and musicians use this drawing as a graphic score. As musicians perform, the artist responds to the music and modifies the emerging picture resultantly. Thus, artist and musicians are communicating within an ongoing improvisation mediated by technology.

Another cross-disciplinary project focused on collaborative processes is *Something Smashing* (Figure 8.1), an initiative developed by author GW along with dancers Alma Lindenhovius and Skye Reynolds. This project bringing artists from dance and music to improvise freely together arose from the observation that, while musicians frequently improvised among themselves and dancers often did the same, they rarely did so in combination. Rather than dancers improvising to music, or musicians supplying a soundtrack to dance, the sessions aim for performers to feel that they are influencing as well as responding to each other's discipline.

The Australian Art Orchestra (Figure 8.2) has long and acclaimed history of exploring the relationship between improvisation and composition, working across disciplines and cultures and using the innovative technologies to create new work and new opportunities for contemporary musicians. Post-genre improvisation lies at the heart of its practice and recent projects include

[3] https://musictechfest.net/project/ann-rosen-sten-olof-hellstrom-the-great-barrier-orchestra-the-knee-cuff-instrument/

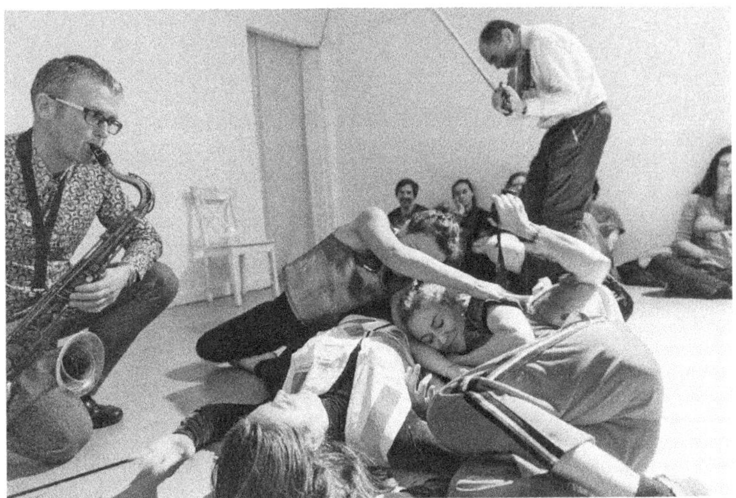

Figure 8.1 "*Something Smashing*, an evening of cross-disciplinary improvisation in Edinburgh, Scotland. Left to right: author GW, Skye Loneragan, Monica de Ioanni, Skye Reynolds, Ken Slaven. Photo credit: Lucas Kao

professional development projects targeted at enhancing the career of young composers/improvisers.[4]

This has been fertile ground for artistic enquiry, raising as many questions as opportunities: for instance, how to switch from interacting with a dancer to interacting with a musician; how to split attention between the visual and the auditory; or how to attend to the physical risks and demands of dance while maintaining a connection to the ongoing music. For both dancers and musicians, this is a new field of practice. Audiences are a combination of individuals who might not otherwise have arrived at the same events, but are brought together by an interest in improvised performance of whatever sort.

[4] http://www.aao.com.au

Figure 8.2 Australian Art Orchestra with Toshmaru Nakamura and Keichiro Shibuya in Yokohama, 2018. Photo credit: 'supplied' "

However, such events frequently have to be defined to others as music events with dance, or as dance events with music. The Great Barrier Orchestra project is described as a "living sound installation"; yet the project features music compositions, sound art works, interdisciplinary collaborations, scores, choreography, and performances. Further development of these exciting directions might be supported by festivals or funding streams dedicated to improvised performance whatever discipline or disciplines it emerges from. This may require redefining milestones or outcomes to reflect the transitory, process-based focus of the improvised oeuvre.

The relationship between composition and improvisation within cross-disciplinary collaborative contexts are to the fore in projects involving graphic scores.

Graphic scores are a particularly popular type of cross-disciplinary creative practice utilising non-conventional musical notation to convey instructions to musicians (Sauer, 2009). Importantly they always involve improvisation of some type. Although the composer of a graphic score will convey instructions about how the score is to be interpreted, improvisational decisions will be made by the performers. For example, musicians are asked to employ improvisational techniques to negotiate the graphic score shown in Figure 8.3 (Ganter and MacDonald, 2018).

In this example performers are asked to treat the red lines as bar lines, the black lines as long notes or long textures, the grey shapes as melodic material. The blue blocks represent granular material. The musicians negotiate the score following specific instructions while making a series of improvisational decisions. Specifically, the black horizontal lines do not indicate a particular note so musicians must choose a note. The position of the black line suggests whether that note is relatively high or low on whatever instrument being played. The last four bars of this piece suggest a series of four long notes, each note one bar long, and each note lower in pitch than the previous. The first note should be relativity high and the last relatively low. The musicians must make other improvised decisions such as volume and timbral quality etc. Thus, the graphic score combines elements of improvisation with elements of predetermined instructions. Another important feature of this project was that the collaboration involved an artist (Josephine Ganter) and a musician (RM) immersing themselves in each other's practice. In doing so the musician was involved in the aesthetic decisions about how the graphic score looked and the artist was equally involved in decisions about what particular musical information was conveyed by the graphic score and how it was performed. These elements of the project necessitated a particular type of improvisational activity in terms of the ongoing discussions between artist and musician. It also helped take the collaborators into new areas of thinking and working.[5]

[5] http://www.woodstockguild.org/PDFs/DrawingSoundCatalog.pdf

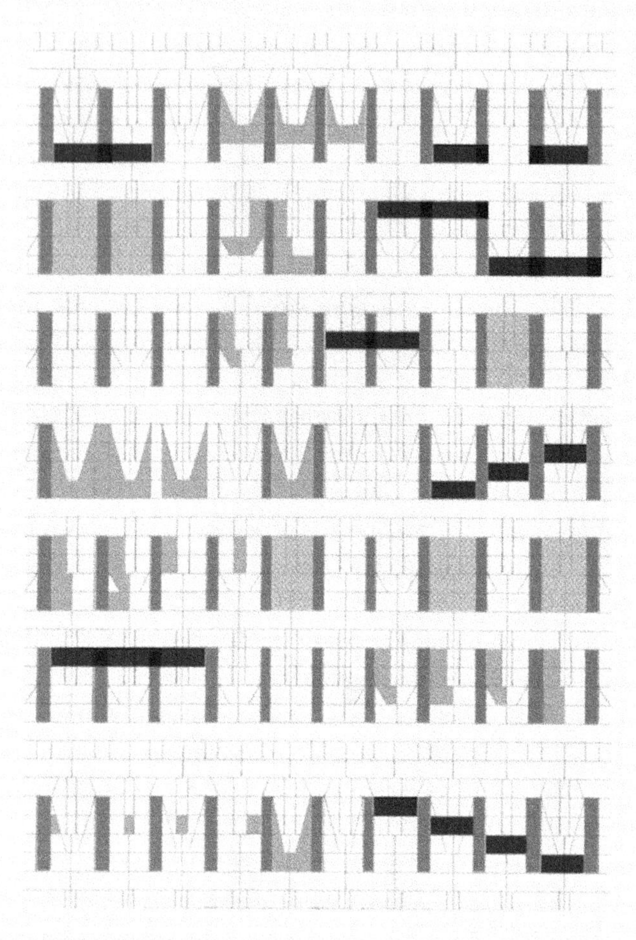

Figure 8.3 Manuscript 2. Graphic score by Josephine Ganter and Raymond MacDonald

When improvisation is viewed as a sophisticated form of social cooperation, there are possible implications for investigating how improvisation functions in organisations since the basic components of improvisation are present in many elements of daily life (chapter 2). Another emerging area of interest, and one with considerable potential for developing new insights about how improvisation functions, is investigating how improvisation can form an integral part of disciplines outside performing arts. It is an important aspect in professions such as medicine, firefighting, law, and politics used continuously but often not acknowledged. For instance, a seminar organised by theorist and improviser Adam Linson for the Concurrent network involved a chef, a professional skateboarder, and an explorer discussing their practice with an explicit focus upon the improvisational elements, highlighting issues such as critical incident decision making and spontaneous generation of novel solutions. In these real-life examples, the ability to make instantaneous decisions when surprise situations arise is crucial. Also, the improvisatory choices made in these moments need to be good decisions as they can quite literally be life or death choices. A fire fighter deciding a route out of a burning building or a surgeon faced with an unexpected development during an operation must improvise their way out of these serious situations.

A research project titled *Into the Key of Law: Transposing Musical Improvisation. The Case of Child Protection in Northern Ireland*[6] considered improvisation as part of the legal process of family courts. It looked at how musical improvisatory practices could be transposed into legal settings (Ramshaw and Stapleton, 2015). These authors note the improvisational practices used by a judge responding to individuals in the courtroom, while interpreting explicit rules of law, shared similar features with musical improvisations in the way in which real-time decisions were made. For example, listening, one of the primary tasks of an improviser, can be viewed as an improvised activity. Also, listening is a crucial part of social interactions of the types described previously.

[6] http://translatingimprovisation.com/ahrc

Improvisation, Community, and Social Practice was a large multi-institutional, international research project based in Canada.[7] Here Ajay Heble and colleagues from a wide range of disciplines (philosophers, musicologists, sociologists, cultural theorists, and literary scholars) explored theoretical and policy issues focusing on how improvisation can be viewed as a social practice with relevance across many areas of society. These projects draw on the observation that improvisation has the potential to shed new light upon how organisations function and inform public policy about the importance of arts in society.

The growth and transformation of improvisatory practice that we anticipate here is certainly to be welcomed as a guarantee of a vibrant and relevant arts scene. It is essential that research in this field takes account of this constant evolution of practice. When we study improvisation, we are not considering a fixed phenomenon; improvisation now is not the same as that practiced a hundred years ago, or twenty years ago, and is unlikely to be consistent with what performers will be doing twenty years hence. All lines of research enquiry should therefore proceed from a statement about how the improvisation is to be understood within a broader field of practice. Indeed, this might be considered a primary means to judge the validity of such research.

Defining improvisation

Chapter 2 focused on definitions and theoretical accounts of improvisation. The importance of offering a pragmatic definition and highlighting key research themes was highlighted. We suggested that improvisation is social, universal, spontaneous, and ambiguous and showed how disparate activities such as two babies improvising or two accomplished improvisers performing could

[7] http://www.improvcommunity.ca/about/research.

share similar features. Various different theories accounting for improvisation were presented including psychodynamic approaches and cognitive approaches, suggesting that, while these theories give a very detailed explanation of improvisation in specific contexts, there is a need for theories to extend their range of convenience to account for the vastly different contexts in which improvisation takes place. Future research should take into account new models and new approaches to improvisation. For example, in chapter 6 we applied personal construct theory to help understand how improvisers talk about their practice. Neuroscience has developed significantly in the past twenty years but there remains a need view improvising as a social phenomenon and new technologies will facilitate brain imaging of people improvising together. This will undoubtedly lead to new insights.

Talking about improvising

In chapter 3 we highlighted the importance of discourse in constructing, challenging, and changing musical identities. It may be useful in light of our arguments in chapter 3 to reflect on how improvisation is taught within music. In mainstream music and dance education, students are typically divided into two streams, namely, creators (composers/choreographers) and executors (musicians/dancers). It is fundamentally expected of creators that they are thinking about, and making decisions regarding, the music or dance they wish to produce. They will be trained to deliver coherent arguments for why the music or dance should be the way they have designed it. In contrast, executors (musicians and dancers) have traditionally been trained to very exacting standards in the execution or realisation of what a composer or choreographer has decided they should produce. They are not typically expected to make choices about what to play, or to exercise their critical faculties in a defence of their own creative choices.

In fine art education, the expectation of creating and justifying work is extended to all students, and defence of one's work is routinely undertaken in a social context of peers in the form of group "crits" of ongoing work. Thus, if a group of students choose to develop work as an improvised performance, they would be expected to discuss what they had done, what shaped their approach to the performance, and whether they had met their objectives for the project etc. In other words, they would be expected to talk about their work, positioning it in the discourses of fine art and of their peers. Improvisation in dance and music typically falls between the artificial stools of composition and performance—not quite seen as either—but tends to be treated as an aspect of performance, and therefore something to be externally assessed as a feat against objective criteria, rather than as a considered creative process on the student's part.

Moving towards an art school model for improvisation in other disciplines would entail not just developing a set of observable skills, but the ability to display critical insight into what students aim to achieve. These may not be defined by a single set of assessment criteria. In art school, innovation is paramount, and the student who produces new work without precedent, and can justify that as a creative choice arising from a process of critical thinking, will excel. The more we can encourage developing improvisers to talk about what they are doing and why, the better we can support the creativity in that process, and the less likely it will be that kneejerk reactions to innovation in improvisation stifle new creative directions.

Implications of a model for decisions in group improvising

In chapter 4 we set out a model for individual decision making within group improvisation. This adds to existing cognitive models that explain improvisation as a solo act by recognising that much of what an improviser in a group may do is essentially responsive rather than a process of continual individual invention. Importantly, this implies that what an improviser does in a group is inevitably constrained by the immediate social context. This chapter proposes that creativity can function as a social process or, in more recent terminology, is *distributed*. Understanding improvisation in these terms changes what we see and access as creative and informs how it can be approached in the cognitive sciences and arts infrastructures.

The model is intended as a means to explain what takes place between improvisers in any context. As such it treats improvisation as a universal behaviour; it is something anyone can do, since the same principles are at play no matter who takes part or for what purpose. However, it also allows for improvisation as a heterogeneous process. Pressing's predominant cognitive model represents improvisation as a single looped process. From this, we might expect that improvisation emerging from such a process to be a relatively constant and undifferentiated affair, to be switched on at the start of a "solo" and switched off at the end. Because our model contains multiple possible circuits, it clearly reflects that any single improvisation is not homogenous. An improvisation can be sharply distinct at different points with radically different inputs from each improviser over its course.

Research to date has not offered much to explain a performance where, for instance, not much happens, then suddenly a great deal happens, and gradually each participant starts doing quite different things from each other until a silence emerges. It is to be hoped that our model could be applied to understanding changes in the course of an improvisation. To this end, it would be useful for future research to consider how the execution of choices within our model might explain the emergence of different features of improvised performances. In particular, the model of choices might be applied to consider how endings are arrived at. This is a significant point of debate among most improvisers and, as noted previously, a key challenge for those seeking to emulate with software what improvisers do.

As a cognitive model the categories of choice we have highlighted also have relevance to the expanding field of interest in developing artificial improvisers (Linson, 2013; Linson, Dobbyn, and Laney, 2012). These are systems that can interact with musicians in a way consistent with the human experience of group improvisation. From our perspective, the important feature of such initiatives is that they seek, through technological means, to realise *group* creativity. Rather than build a machine that will supplant musicians and generate music itself, they proceed from the understanding that improvisation is fundamentally interactive. Some of the strategies outlined in our model are similar to components of some of those systems (e.g., Murray-Rust and Smaill, 2011).

However, a decision process programmed into software can be expected not make mistakes or produce uncertain results, but rather to follow algorithmic rules precisely. Those decisions we have abstracted and incorporated into the model were described by improvisers after the event. Most musicians comment, when trying to describe their improvising, that it is often an instinctive or unconscious process, and that accidents, unintentional or non-deliberate actions, are also part of what goes on. If analogous strategies can be tried by both humans and machines, we have the potential to consider how they are generative either when applied "purely," by computer software, or with the "imperfect noise" that one might expect in any human improviser.

Creativity is one of the most revered features of all artistic activity. Treating it as a rare and powerful characteristic, without which improvisation will be pointless or lacking value, can be off-putting for people wanting to give improvisation a go. Supporting creative practice in these terms may require radical transformations in arts infrastructure. Funding or commissioning, curating, and copyright are all keystones of the arts as a profession that are typically geared to supporting art produced by individuals. Grants are most easily administered if awarded to one person and typically ask for a lead applicant. Contracts for performances or recordings are most straightforward if signed by one person and intellectual property rights may become a minefield where no one person can be seen as their creator.

There are also important implications for supporting access to performance practice. Because the creativity of group improvisation emerges through interaction, anyone in an improvising group will find themselves part of a creative process, generating unprecedented music even if they do not feel that they personally have invented any of what was played. This type of inclusive creative group work can be facilitated by a teacher or ensemble leader to encourage wary or self-conscious individuals into participation. If they are allowed initially to experience the enjoyment of being within a group improvisation, without feeling individually responsible, they can begin to consciously influence the process whenever they feel comfortable doing so. By training and encouraging developing improvisers (or highly experienced ones) to be more responsive to the improvisers around them, and to defer creative responsibility to the group rather than themselves, we are more likely to foster the emergence of startling new music, dance, or performance art that must be celebrated as the achievement of an ensemble. This all suggests a need for funding streams that look to support the interaction of improvisers in order to arrive at novel performance, rather than commissioning new objects that are understood to be created by individuals.

The myth of shared understanding: the new psychology of improvisation

Psychological research into improvisation characteristically assumes that improvisers must share an understanding of what they are doing. In chapter 5, we argued that shared understanding is less important to the success of improvisation than the investment of each person in the process; indeed, that divergence in understandings is more likely to generate novel outcomes from group improvisation. The studies described in chapter 5 open diverse avenues for future research.

Our research was innovative in considering how more than two people improvise together, despite this being how most improvisation takes place. Since responses to others are central, there is a considerable step change from a duo to a trio in that there is now a choice of who to respond to, and an awareness that another improviser might be responding to another group member rather than to oneself. Yet trios are scarcely the largest format available. It will therefore be vital to establish how the processes of constructing musical meaning vary as group size increases. For instance, within the larger ensembles that are increasingly a feature of contemporary improvisation, are there subgroups during an improvisation whose understandings of what is going on are more convergent amongst themselves than with the rest of the group?

Another fruitful line of enquiry would be to conceptualise more precisely the understanding between music therapists and their clients. If divergent understandings can generate the novel behaviours that might constitute a clinical breakthrough, what focus should be given in the clinical process to improvising that the therapist does *not* seek to understand, or understands differently from the client? In terms of practice, it would also be valuable to explore how can we support divergent understandings between improvisers in the long term, to avoid improvising relationships becoming stale. We need to understand how divergent understandings interact in improvised practice, or what an optimal balance of understanding and misunderstanding might be achieved.

In all the areas we have identified where improvisation might have useful applications, there is a need to reflect upon the new understanding of improvisation that we have expounded in this book. Beyond music, it would be informative to understand whether similar processes of construction can explain spontaneous creative practice in other artforms, or indeed might underlie other non-verbal spontaneous interactions such as that in team sports. The objectives of diverse group activities that can be seen as involving non-verbal improvisation (e.g., team sports, dancing, online gaming, etc.) can be achieved even if those involved do not share precisely the same understandings of those objectives. Our arguments suggest that the focus for research in these fields should not be on how an individual improvises in the sports field, dancefloor, or internet but instead to consider what makes a team or group behave in a spontaneous, creative, and non-verbal way. Considering each person involved as someone with bespoke expectations and the means to predict situations, and considering the group's behaviour as something that can only have arisen from that combination of people rather than as a result of the input of any one of them, will provide new insights.

Furthermore, despite decades in which improvisation has burgeoned as a feature of arts practice, performing and composing are typically engaged with as separate activities. Rather than thinking of group creativity in improvisation as an aggregate of individual contributions, we have argued that much of what can be appreciated as creative may emerge through understandings that are not shared, without having been the intention of any one member of that group, something greater than the sum of its parts or participants. The creative process must come to be seen in most improvised practice as an outcome of the engine of the group. This requires a fundamental rethinking of how we value performance.

Supporting improvisational development

We have set out an innovative framework for understanding and evaluating how an individual develops as an improviser. This should be regarded as a separate strand of development from progression as a musician or other performer within one or another genre. In proposing new virtuosities, we delineate the spectrum of transferable attributes that are honed through continued practice in improvisation. These are essentially critical, creative, and social skills. All of these skills are widely hailed as positive capacities to be fostered in individuals, demonstrating the potential benefits of dedicated training in improvisational practice and offering a challenge to curriculum development.

If creative capacity for improvisation is to be developed it might be expected to be particularly nurtured in social contexts. The formation and testing of individual ways to predict events can best be practiced through response and social interaction; in other words, in the presence of others. Dance is primarily taught in groups; musical education in the UK takes place via both social (classroom, ensemble) and individual (practice, tuition) settings, while visual arts teaching is characterised by a particular emphasis on one-to-one teaching and individual practice. In music and visual arts pedagogy, it would be valuable to consider how social learning and opportunities to create spontaneously together can be maximised, to provide learners with the best chance to develop their own robust constructs for taking part in improvisation. During primary, secondary, or tertiary education, children and young people have an unparalleled opportunity to improvise with a fixed group of peers over a number of years. This is something that can be extremely difficult to achieve and sustain in either community or professional contexts in the present day, compared with the informal learning environments described, for instance, by the interviewees in MacGlone and MacDonald (2017) or observed among developing rock musicians by Green (2002).

Encouraging and supporting learners to consider how well they are able to predict what those around them are doing, even as those people change and develop, should be a priority for arts education. This requires that teaching supports the development of musical relationships rather than simply the playing of music. In artforms where individuals must balance their own approaches, tastes, and objectives with those of their collaborators, social processes are vital to success. Educators should seek to help students to think about, and value, what they perceive others to be doing; to reflect on how their participation in group improvisation confirms or refutes their expectations and to consider how it might go differently next time. Encouraging students to discuss their practice with each other is another important approach, as is the encouragement of cross-disciplinary project work. This will bring students into the widest range of improvising contexts. The broader the range of improvisers they encounter and interact with, the more developed their systems of constructs for improvising will become.

That is not to say that one-to-one teaching has little to offer development as an improviser. It is also worth considering the widespread bifurcation in music education between the teaching of creative practice as composition, and that of executing music as performance. Creative performance is not well supported in this system. It could be argued that improvisation tends to be taught primarily as an aspect of performance, a different way of making music happen rather than focusing on what that music is. Yet the teaching of composition or choreography, which perhaps has more in common with visual arts pedagogy (e.g., in the development of a portfolio of work), is at least as appropriate to what improvisers do, if we understand the objective of improvising to be the generation of novel and rewarding music.

Composition teaching in higher education has been characterised as a process toward shared goals through problem finding and problem solving, reciprocity, and collaborative dialogue, with possible solutions discussed, negotiated, and trialled (Barrett, 2006; Barrett and Gromko, 2007). Such a process of trial and self-critique is likely to be an important means to support the developing improviser towards the individually distinctive and innovative practice to which composers, choreographers, and visual artists are expected to aspire, particularly in an era with such easy access to the means to record improvised performances for later reflection. In particular, learning to formulate, refine, trust, and evolve one's own criteria for successful improvising is vital, and entirely consistent with this model of education (Johansen, 2018).

The focus of assessment on individual performance, for instance in grade exams in music, is problematic as a means of evaluating improvisational development. Alternative strategies such as assessment of group performance or peer critique represent more appropriate ways of measuring progress as an improviser. Virkkula (2016), for instance, has recently pointed to the potential for informal learning in jazz education through workshop learning with professional musicians, where students have a high level of responsibility for the content and evaluation of learning outcomes. Hickey (2015) has mapped the practices of leading educators in free improvisation at a tertiary level and identified a heavily group-based learning environment. Nevertheless, assessing creative contribution to a group process can represent a challenge for the assessor, and further research in this area towards guidelines for assessment practice would be a useful contribution.

In short, we anticipate a revolution in arts teaching and community arts that sees performers from many disciplines learning together how to arrive at startlingly different work that exceeds all their expectations. This can only be a rewarding and thrilling eventuality for all those who value artistic innovation.

Music, health, and well-being

Chapter 7 outlined various approaches to improvisation and music, health, and well-being. While there is a growing body of research highlighting the efficacy of improvisation for positive psychological outcomes, there is still a need to understand in more detail the processes and outcomes of improvisation interventions in contemporary contexts, particularly those outwith the music therapy area. Future research should consider how improvisation may also have preventive effects. For example, engaging in improvisation may slow down cognitive and physical deterioration associated with Alzheimer's or Parkinson's disease or stop symptoms of depression from developing. Future research should investigate this issue in both clinical and non-clinical contexts including music therapy, community, and educational settings. Mixed-method approaches using both quantitative and qualitative techniques offer the possibility of holistic accounts of the lived experience of improvisation (MacDonald and Wilson, 2014). Social and psychological research methods combined with musicological analysis is another way of assessing the health implications of improvising. For example, can some improvisations be characterised as healthy while others as unhealthy? Another recent development is a growth of interest in the relationship between improvisation and health for musicians and artists outwith the clinical profession. A recent edition of a monthly music magazine, *The Wire*, featured an article investigating the relationship between improvisation and mental health (Barre, 2018). This article, although not exclusively focused on improvisation, centred around the use of music in hospitals for individuals with mental health problems and included a discussion of improvisation and of graphic scores, field recordings, and universal musicality, once again highlighting the extent to which the relationship between improvisation and health has entered public awareness.

What next?

We suggest that improvisation is one of the most exciting ways to perform, or to be creative with others. There is no sign of societies running out of new ideas for how to improvise, or what to improvise, or of what improvisation can look like. Indeed, we may be returning to a golden age before fixed ideas of musical or artistic products took hold. What we hope this book does is instil and communicate some of the excitement we feel when improvising, or when thinking about what improvisers must be doing. These ideas are not simply entertaining; improvisation is a hugely significant psychological feat accomplished by everyone, yet without garnering commensurate attention from psychological theory and research.

We hope that the ideas we have put forward in our research inspire others to ask how we might take these ideas further, or how looking at improvisation might inform understandings of other areas of human endeavour. Technological advances that allow groups of improvisers to have their brains scanned simultaneously as they improvise together will enable a more social understanding of how we collaborate in real time. However, we would also like to see more consideration of why improvisers describe their practice in the way they do and more focus on why combinations of improvisers with different ideas produce the improvisations they do, instead of more studies on individuals with the same conception. Further consideration and application of social constructionist ideas of language will help pluralistic models of quality in improvisation to thrive.

The rise of the virtuoso improviser, a practitioner who can adapt themselves to working across different disciplines collaboratively, will see new types of artwork emerge and new types of practice. We therefore see huge potential for education and community initiatives that prioritise the nurturing and fulfilment of individual creative visions from their outset through reflective participation in group music making. Students should be able to take a degree in improvisation, where the process-based aspects of creative collaboration are valued more than the outcomes. Fine art students should study alongside music or literature students to develop specialist knowledge of improvisational practice. Such initiatives might leave us not just culturally better off, but in better social, mental, and physical health. Our ideas must inevitably be challenged by where improvisation is going and what others make of it; but we look forward to keeping up with unforeseen developments that the great creative ferment of improvisation produces.

The title of this book emphasises the process of improvisation, *the art of becoming*. It is in these processes that we think the future of improvisation will blossom. Improvisation is universally accessible, and it surrounds us and helps define who we are. It provides a catalyst for the ebb and flow of daily life. It is an essential artistic process whose use is blossoming around the world. Technological advances will combine with improvisational processes to facilitate collaboration in ways we have not yet contemplated. A virtual, global, cross-disciplinary orchestra of improvisers does not seem too far-fetched given the evidence we have presented within this book.

Improvisation is not just the art of the becoming; it is also the art of the unrepeatable, ephemeral moments that are not just staging posts to a destination but important events and movements in their own right. Their very ephemerality and unrepeatability mean that they can be precious and life changing or mundane and boring, frivolous and playful and joyous and ecstatic. In the moments of improvisation, we have opportunities: to explore our identity; to connect with other people; to make conceptual breakthroughs and gain new insights; to develop our confidence or self-esteem; to be understood; to be misunderstood; and still to have fun within an artistic and expressive environment. When we improvise, we make choices about what to play and when to play, and these choices mirror fundamental life processes: improvisation is life, and life is improvisation. The more we improvise the richer our view of the world becomes. We have attempted to proselytise about improvisation, to be evidence-based about its merits but not fundamentalist about its function, because we are enthralled by the possibilities of what might become of this art.

References

Adamowicz, E. (1998). *Surrealist collage in text and image: Dissecting the exquisite corpse*. Cambridge: Cambridge University Press.

Aebersold, J. (2012). *How to play jazz & improvise*. New Albany, IN: Jamey Aebersold Jazz.

Alluri, V., Toiviainen, P., Jääskeläinen, I., Glerean, E., Sams, M., and Brattico, E. (2012). Large-scale brain networks emerge from dynamic processing of musical timbre, key and rhythm. *Neuroimage, 59*, 3677–3689. doi:10.1016/j.neuroimage.2011.11.019.

Alvin, J. (1978). *Music therapy for the autistic child*. Oxford: Oxford University Press.

Amabile, T. M. (1996). *Creativity in context: Update to the social psychology of creativity*. New York: Westview Press.

Arthurs, T. (2015). Improvised music in Berlin 2012–13: A brief ethnographic portrait. *Critical Studies in Improvisation / Études critiques en improvisation, 10*(2), 1–18. doi:10.21083/csieci.v10i2.3584.

Bailey, D. (1993). *Improvisation: Its nature and practice in music*. Boston, MA: Da Capo.

Banister, P., Burman, E., Parker, I., Taylor, M., and Tindall, C. (Eds.). (1998). *Qualitative methods in psychology*. Buckingham, UK: Open University Press.

Barre, T. (2018). Music and mental health. *Wire, 415*, 34–40.

Barrett, M. (2006). "Creative collaboration": An "eminence" study of teaching and learning in music composition. *Psychology of Music, 34*(2), 195–218. doi:10.1177/0305735606061852.

Barrett, M. S., and Gromko, J. E. (2007). Provoking the muse: A case study of teaching and learning in music composition. *Psychology of Music, 35*(2), 213–230. doi:10.1177/0305735607070305.

Barron, S., Dube, W., and Palazzo Grassi. (1997). *German expressionism: Art and society*. England: Thames and Hudson.

Beaty, R. E. (2015). The neuroscience of musical improvisation. *Neuroscience & Biobehavioral Reviews, 51*(0), 108–117. http://dx.doi.org/10.1016/j.neubiorev.2015.01.004.

Becker, H. S. (1984). *Art worlds*. London: University of California Press.

Beil, R., and Kraut, P. (2012). *A house full of music: Strategies in music and art*. Darmstadt: Hatje Cantz.

Berkowitz, A. L. (2010). *The improvising mind: Cognition and creativity in the musical moment*. Oxford: Oxford University Press.

Berliner, P. F. (1994). *Thinking in Jazz: The infinite art of improvisation*. Chicago: University of Chicago Press.

Blowers, G. H., and Bacon Shone, J. (1994). On detecting the differences in jazz: A reassessment of comparative methods of measuring perceptual. *Empirical Studies of the Arts*, *12*(1), 41–58.

Borden, W. (2009). Contemporary psychodynamic theory and practice. Lyceum Books.

Borgo, D. (2006). *Sync or swarm: Improvising music in a complex age*. New York: Bloomsbury.

Born, G., Lewis, E., and Straw, W. (2017). *Improvisation and social aesthetics: Improvisation, community, and social practice*. Durham, NC: Duke University Press.

Born, G. (2017). "From network bands to ubiquitous computing: Rich Gold and the social aesthetics of interactivity." In *Improvisation and social aesthetics*, edited by G. Born, E. Lewis, and W. Straw, 91–109. Durham, NC: Duke University Press.

Canonne, C., and Aucouturier, J.-J. (2016). Play together, think alike: Shared mental models in expert music improvisers. *Psychology of Music*, *44*(3), 544–558. doi:10.1177/0305735615577406.

Canonne, C., and Garnier, N. (2011). A model for collective free improvisation. In *Mathematics and computation in music: Third international conference, MCM 2011, Paris, France, June 15–17, 2011. Proceedings*, edited by C. Agon, M. Andreatta, G. Assayag, E. Amiot, J. Bresson, and J. Mandereau, 29–41. Berlin, Heidelberg: Springer.

Clarke, E. F., and Doffman, M. (2018). *Distributed creativity: Collaboration and improvisation in contemporary music*. Oxford: Oxford University Press.

Cochrane, T. (2017). Group flow. In *The Routledge companion to embodied music interaction*, edited by M. Lesaffre, P.-J. Maes, and M. Leman, 133–140. London: Taylor & Francis Group.

Coltrane, J. (1995). *The heavyweight champion: The complete Atlantic recordings*. New York: Atlantic Records.

Corbett, J. (2016). *A listener's guide to free improvisation*. Chicago: University of Chicago Press.

Csikszentmihalyi, M. (1991). *Flow: The psychology of optimal experience*. New York: Harper Perennial.

Dean, R. T., and Bailes, F. (2016). Cognitive processes in musical improvisation. In *The Oxford handbook of critical improvisation studies*, Vol. 1, edited by G. E. Lewis and B. Piekut. Oxford: Oxford University Press.

Dean, R. (1989). *Creative improvisation*. Milton Keynes: Open University Press.

Deutsch, D., Henthorn, T., and Lapidis, R. (2011). Illusory transformation from speech to song. *Journal of the Acoustical Society of America, 129*, 2245–2252.

Dietrich, A. (2004). The cognitive neuroscience of creativity. *Psychonomic Bulletin & Review, 11*(6), 1011–1026.

Donnay, G. F., Rankin, S. K., Lopez-Gonzalez, M., Jiradejvong, P., and Limb, C. J. (2014). Neural substrates of interactive musical improvisation: An fMRI study of "trading fours" in jazz. *PLoS ONE, 9*(2), e88665. doi:10.1371/journal.pone.0088665.

Erkkilä, J., Gold, C., Fachner, J., Ala-Ruona, E., Punkanen, M., and Vanhala, M. (2008). The effect of improvisational music therapy on the treatment of depression: Protocol for a randomised controlled trial. *BMC Psychiatry, 8*, 50.

Erkkilä, J., Punkanen, M., Fachner, J., Ala-Ruona, E., Pöntiö, I., Tervaniemi, M., et al. (2011). Individual music therapy for depression: Randomised controlled trial. *The British Journal of Psychiatry, 199*(2), 132–139. doi:10.1192/bjp.bp.110.085431.

Ferlaino, C. (2018). Confluences: Folk wisdom in contemporary music, PhD Thesis, University of Edinburgh.

Eyles, J. (2003). Evan Parker. Retrieved from http://www.allaboutjazz.com/evan-parker-by-john-eyles.php#.UqzMRc1aH4o.

Fachner, J., Gold, C., and Erkkila, J. (2013). Music therapy modulates fronto-temporal activity in rest-EEG in depressed clients. *Brain Topography, 26*(2), 338–354.

Ferand, E. T. (1938). *Die Improvisation in der Musik: Eine entwicklungsgeschichtliche und psychologische Untersuchung*. Zurich: Rhein-Verlag.

Fischlin, D., and Heble, A. (Eds.). (2004). *The other side of nowhere: Jazz improvisation and communities in dialogue*. Middletown, CT: Wesleyan University Press.

Fisher, E. (2010). Contemporary technology discourse. In *Media and new capitalism in the digital age*, edited by E. Fisher, 29–41. New York: Palgrave Macmillan.

Fransella, F., Bell, R., and Bannister, D. (2004). *A manual for repertory grid technique*: Chichester, West Sussex, England: John Wiley & Sons.

Freeman, P. (2010). Wadada Leo Smith uncut. *The Wire, 312*, 40–47.

Gaines, B. R., and Shaw, M. L. G. (2018). Rep plus: Conceptual representation software. Calgary: University of Calgary. Retrieved from http://cpsc.ucalgary.ca/~gaines/repplus.

Ganter, J., and MacDonald, R. (2018). Manuscript 2, Under Bridge Gate: Exhibition of graphic scores. Glasgow: The Briggait.

Gentner, D., and Stevens, A. L. (1983). *Mental models*. Hillsdale, NJ: L. Erlbaum Associates.

Giddens, A. (2001). *Modernity and self identity*. Cambridge: Polity.

Gilbert, N., and Mulkay, M. (1984). *Opening Pandora's box: A sociological analysis of scientists' discourse*. Cambridge: Cambridge University Press.

Gilboa A., Bodner E., and Amir D. (2006). Emotional communicability in improvised music: The case of music therapists. *Journal of Music Therapy*, *43*(3), 198–225. 10.1093/jmt/43.3.198.

Green, L. (2002). Exposing the gendered discourse of music education. *Feminism and Psychology*, *12*(2), 137–144.

Hargreaves, D. J., MacDonald, R. A. R., and Miell, D. (2005). How do people communicate using music? In *Musical communication*, edited by D. Miell, R. A. R. MacDonald, and D. J. Hargreaves, 1–25. Oxford: Oxford University Press.

Hargreaves, D., and Lamont, A. (2017). *The psychology of musical development*. Cambridge: Cambridge University Press.

Hart, E., and Di Blasi, Z. (2013). Combined flow in musical jam sessions: A pilot qualitative study. *Psychology of Music*, *43*(2), 275–290. doi:10.1177/0305735613502374.

Hayes, L. (2017). Sound, electronics, and music: A radical and hopeful experiment in early music education. *Computer Music Journal*, *41*(3), 36–49.

Hickey, M. (2015). Learning from the experts: A study of free-improvisation pedagogues in university settings. *Journal of Research in Music Education*, *62*(4), 425–445. doi:10.1177/0022429414556319.

Hickey, M., Ankney, K., Healy, D., and Gallo, D. (2016). The effects of group free improvisation instruction on improvisation achievement and improvisation confidence. *Music Education Research*, *18*(2), 127–141. doi:10.1080/14613808.2015.1016493.

Hill, J. (2017). Incorporating improvisation into classical music performance. In *Musicians in the Making: Pathways to Creative Performance*, edited by J. Rink, H. Gaunt and A. Williamon, 222–240. New York: Oxford University Press.

Holbrook, M. B., and Huber, J. (1983). Detecting the differences in jazz: A comparison of methods for assessing perceptual veridicality in applied aesthetics. *Empirical Studies of the Arts*, *1*(1), 35–53. doi:10.2190/pjap-rqdm-02pv-e25v.

Holbrook, M., and Huber, J. (1979). The spatial representation of responses toward jazz: Applications of consumer esthetics to mapping the market for music. *Journal of Jazz Studies*, *5*(2), 3–22.

Ignatidou, S. (2013). Mohammad: Secrets and lyres. *Wire*, March 2013.

Jeannerod, M. (2003). The mechanism of self-recognition in humans. *Behavioural Brain Research*, 142, 1–15.

Johansen, G. G. (2018). Explorational instrumental practice: An expansive approach to the development of improvisation competence. *Psychology of Music*, *46*(1), 49–65. doi:10.1177/0305735617695657.

Johnson-Laird, P. N. (2002). How jazz musicians improvise. *Music Perception, 19*(3), 415–442. doi:10.1525/mp.2002.19.3.415.

Kelley, R. (2010). *Thelonious Monk: The life and times of an American original.* New York: The Free Press.

Kelly, G. (2002). *The psychology of personal constructs: Theory and personality*, Vol. 1. London: Routledge.

Kennedy, C. (2013). Stop and listen to the world. *Music Works, 115.*

Kennedy, M. (2009, 30 July). Organist wins battle for recognition for "A whiter shade of pale" riff. *The Guardian.* Retrieved from https://www.theguardian.com/music/2009/jul/30/lords-ruling-whiter-shade-pale.

Lesaffre, M., Maes, P.-J., and Leman, M. (2017). *The Routledge companion to embodied music interaction.* London: Routledge.

Levy, R. A., & Ablon, J. S. (Eds.). (2009). Handbook of evidence-based psychodynamic psychotherapy: Bridging the gap between science and practice. New Jersey, United States: Humana Press.

Lewis, G. E. (2009). A power stronger than itself: The AACM and American experimental music. Chicago: University of Chicago Press.

Lewis, G. E. (2000). Too many notes: Computers, complexity, and culture in Voyager. *Leonardo Music Journal, 10*, 33–39. doi:10.1162/096112100570585.

Lewis, G. E. (2002). Improvised Music after 1950: Afrological and Eurological perspectives. *Black Music Research Journal, 22*, 215–246. doi:10.2307/1519950.

Limb, C. J., and Braun, A. R. (2008). Neural Substrates of Spontaneous Musical Performance: An fMRI Study of Jazz Improvisation. PLoS ONE, *3*(2), e1679. https://doi.org/10.1371/journal.pone.0001679.

Linson, A. (2013). The expressive stance: Intentionality, expression, and machine art. *International Journal of Machine Consciousness, 5*(02), 195–216.

Linson, A., Dobbyn, C., and Laney, R. (2012). *Critical issues in evaluating freely improvising interactive music systems.* Paper presented at the Third International Conference on Computational Creativity, Dublin.

Lochhead, J. I. (1994). Performance practice in the indeterminate works of John Cage. *Performance Practice Review, 7*(2). doi:10.5642/perfpr.199407.02.11.

MacDonald, R. A., and Miell, D. (2002). Music for individuals with special needs: A catalyst for developments in identity, communication, and musical ability: Oxford: Oxford University Press.

MacDonald, R. A., and Wilson, G. B. (2005). Musical identities of professional jazz musicians: A focus group investigation. *Psychology of Music, 33*(4), 395–417. doi:10.1177/0305735605056151.

MacDonald, R. A., and Wilson, G. B. (2006). Constructions of jazz: How jazz musicians present their collaborative musical practice. *Musicae Scientiae, 10*(1), 59–83. doi:10.1177/102986490601000104.

MacDonald, R. A., and Wilson, G. B. (2014). Musical improvisation and health: A review. *Psychology of Well-Being, 4*(1), 20. http://www.psywb.com/content/4/1/20

MacDonald, R. A., and Wilson, G. B. (2016). Billy Connolly, Daniel Barenboim, Willie Wonka, Jazz Bastards, and the Universality of Improvisation. In *The Oxford handbook of critical improvisation studies*, edited by B. Piekut and G. Lewis, 103–120. Oxford: Oxford University Press.

MacDonald, R. A., Wilson, G. B., and Miell, D. (2012). Improvisation as a creative process within contemporary music. In *Musical imaginations: Multidisciplinary perspectives on creativity, performance, and perception*, edited by D. J. Hargreaves, D. Miell, and R. A. R. MacDonald, 242–255. Oxford: Oxford University Press.

MacDonald, R., Hargreaves, D. J., and Miell, D. (Eds.). (2017). *The Oxford handbook of musical identities*. Oxford: Oxford University Press.

MacDonald, R., Hargreaves, D. J., and Miell, D. (Eds.). (2002). *Musical identities*. Oxford: Oxford University Press.

MacGlone, U., and MacDonald, R. (2017). Learning to improvise, improvising to learn: A qualitative study of learning processes in improvising musicians. In *Distributed creativity: Collaboration and improvisation in contemporary music*, edited by E. F. Clarke and M. Doffman, 278–294. New York: Oxford University Press.

McGinn, K. L., and Keros, A. T. (2002). Improvisation and the logic of exchange in socially embedded transactions. *Administrative Science Quarterly, 47*(3), 442–473.

Merriam, Alan P. (1964). *The anthropology of music*. Evanston, IL: Northwestern University Press.

Miller, S. (2013). *Cuban flute style: Interpretation and improvisation*. Lanham, MD: Scarecrow Press.

Mitchell, L., and MacDonald, R. (2012). Music and pain: Evidence from experimental perspectives. In *Music, health, and well-being*, edited by R. A. MacDonald, G. Kreutz, and L. Mitchell, 230–239. Oxford: Oxford University Press.

Monson, I. (1996). *Saying something: Jazz improvisation and interaction*. Chicago: University of Chicago Press.

Monson, I. T. (2007). *Freedom sounds: Civil rights call out to jazz and Africa*. Oxford: Oxford University Press.

Morris, Joe. (2012). *Perpetual frontier: The properties of free music*. Stony Creek, CT: Riti.

Morris, L. B. (2017). *The art of Conduction: A Conduction® workbook*. New York: Karma.

Murray-Rust, D., and Smaill, A. (2011). Towards a model of musical interaction and communication. *Artificial Intelligence, 175*(9), 1697–1721. doi:https://doi.org/10.1016/j.artint.2011.01.002.

Nachmanovitch, S. (2019). *The Art of Is: Improvising as a Way of Life Novato.* CA: New World Library.

Nettl, B., and Russell, M. (Eds.). (2008). *In the course of performance: Studies in the world of musical improvisation.* Chicago & London: University of Chicago Press.

Nicholson, S. (2004). *Ella Fitzgerald: The complete biography.* London: Routledge.

Nooshin, L. (2003). Improvisation as "Other": Creativity, knowledge, and power—The case of Iranian classical music. *Journal of the Royal Musical Association, 128*(2), 242–296.

Nordoff, P., and Robbins, C. (1965). *Music therapy for handicapped children: Investigations and experiences.* New York: Rudolph Steiner Publications.

Norgaard, M. (2011). Descriptions of improvisational thinking by artist-level jazz musicians. *Journal of Research in Music Education, 59*(2), 109–127. doi:10.1177/0022429411405669.

Norgaard, M. (2014). How jazz musicians improvise: The central role of auditory and motor patterns. *Music Perception, 31*(3), 271–287. doi:10.1525/mp.2014.31.3.271.

Novack, C. J. (1990). *Sharing the dance: Contact improvisation and American culture.* Madison: University of Wisconsin Press.

Oldham, J. M., Skodol, A. E., and Bender, D. S. (2014). *The American psychiatric publishing textbook of personality disorders*, 2nd ed. Washington, DC: American Psychiatric Publishing.

Oliveros, P. (2005). *Deep listening: A composer's sound practice.* New York: iUniverse.

Palmer, C. M. (2016). Instrumental jazz improvisation development. *Journal of Research in Music Education, 64*(3), 360–378. doi:10.1177/0022429416664897.

Paranjape, W. (2012). Khyal, improvisation, and social change. *Critical Studies in Improvisation / Études critiques en improvisation, 8*(1).

Parker, E. (2009). Saxophone solos. London: Psi Records.

Petinger, P. (1998). *Bill Evans: How my heart sings.* Yale University Press.

Pickering, Andrew. (1995). *The mangle of practice: Time, agency, and science.* Chicago: University of Chicago Press.

Piekut, Benjamin. (2011). Introduction: What was experimentalism? In *Experimentalism otherwise: The New York avant-garde and its limits*, 1–19. Berkeley: University of California Press.

Poikonen, H., Toiviainen, P., Tervaniemi, M. (2018). Naturalistic music and dance: Cortical phase synchrony in musicians and dancers. *PLoS ONE, 13*(4): e0196065. https://doi.org/10.1371/journal.pone.0196065.

Pothoulaki, M., MacDonald, R. A. R., Flowers, P., Stamataki, E., Filiopoulos, V., Stamatiadis, D., and Stathakis, C. P. (2008). An investigation of the effects of music on anxiety and pain perception in patients undergoing haemodialysis treatment. *Journal of Health Psychology, 13*(7), 912–920. doi:10.1177/1359105308095065.

Potter, J., and Edwards, D. (1992). *Discursive psychology*. London: Sage.

Potter, J., and Wetherell, M. (1987). *Discourse and social psychology: Beyond attitudes and behaviour*. London: Sage.

Pras, A., Schober, M. F., and Spiro, N. (2017). What about their performance do free jazz improvisers agree upon? A case study. *Frontiers in Psychology, 8*(966). doi:10.3389/fpsyg.2017.00966.

Pressing, J. (1987). Improvisation: Methods and models. In *Generative processes in music*, edited by J. Sloboda, 129–178. Oxford: Oxford University Press.

Pressing, J. (1998). Psychological constraints on improvisational expertise and communication. In *In the course of performance: Studies in the world of musical improvisation*, edited by B. Nettl and M. Russell, 47–67. Chicago: University of Chicago Press.

Pressing, J. (2002). Free jazz and the avant-garde. In *The Cambridge companion to jazz*, edited by M. Cooke and D. Horn, 202–216. Cambridge: Cambridge University Press.

Prévost, E. (1995). *No sound is innocent: AMM and the practice of self-invention*. London: Cupola.

Priestley, M. (1985). *Music therapy in action*. St. Louis, MO: MMB Music.

Puchta, C., and Potter, J. (2002). Manufacturing individual opinions: Market research focus groups and the discursive psychology of evaluation. *British Journal of Social Psychology, 41*(3), 345–363. doi:10.1348/014466602760344250.

Ramshaw, S., and Stapleton, P. (2015). Un-remembering: Countering law's archive. Improvisation as social practice. In *Law, violence, memory: Uncovering the counter-archive*, edited by S. Motha and H. van Rijswijk, 50–69. London: Routledge.

Rofe, M., and Geelhoed, E. (2017). Composing for a latency-rich environment. *Journal of Music, Technology, and Education, 10*(2–3), 231–256.

Rogoff, B. (2005). *The cultural nature of human development*. Oxford: Oxford University Press.

Rolvsjord, R., Gold, C., and Stige, B. (2005). Research rigour and therapeutic flexibility: Rationale for a therapy manual developed for a randomised controlled trial. *Nordic Journal of Music Therapy, 14*(1), 15–32. doi:10.1080/08098130509478122.

Rose S.D. (2017) The *lived experience of improvisation: In music learning and life*. Chicago: Intellect.

Ross, A. (2009). *The rest is noise: Listening to the twentieth century*. New York: Harper Perennial.

Rowell, Charles Henry. (2004). "Words don't go there": An interview with Fred Moten. *Callaloo, 27*(4) (Fall) , 953–966.

Rush, S. (2017). *Free jazz, harmolodics and Ornette Coleman*. London: Routledge.

Ryle, G. (1949). *The concept of mind*. Chicago: University of Chicago Press.

Ryle, G. (1976). Improvisation. *Mind, 85*(337), 69–83.

Sauer, T. (2009). *Notations 21*. New York: Mark Batty.

Saunders, J. (2009). Interview with Evan Parker. In *The Ashgate research companion to experimental music*, edited by J. Saunders, 331–336. Farnham: Ashgate.

Sawyer, R. (2008). *Group genius: The creative power of collaboration*. New York: BasicBooks.

Sawyer, R. (2012). *Explaining creativity: The science of human innovation*, 2nd ed. Oxford: Oxford University Press.

Sawyer, R. (2013). *Zig zag: The surprising path to greater creativity*. Hoboken, NJ: Wiley.

Sawyer. (2006). Group creativity: Musical performance and collaboration. *Psychology of Music, 34*(2), 148–165. doi:10.1177/0305735606061850.

Schober, M. F., and Spiro, N. (2014). Jazz improvisers' shared understanding: A case study. *Frontiers in Psychology, 5*. doi:10.3389/fpsyg.2014.00808.

Schütz, M. (2012). *Improvisation in jazz: "Stream of ideas"—Analysis of jazz piano-improvisations*. Paper presented at the 12th International Conference on Music Perception and Cognition & 8th Triennial Conference of the European Society for the Cognitive Sciences of Music, Thessaloniki, Greece.

Sibelius, J. (1919). Interview with Berlingske Tidende, 10 June 1919. Cited at: *Jean Sibelius: In his own words*. http://www.sibelius.fi/english/omin_sanoin/ominsanoin_16.htm

Skewes-McFerran, K., and Wigram, T. (2002). A review of current practice in group music therapy improvisations. *British Journal of Music Therapy, 16*(1), 46–55.

Smith, C., Viljoen, J. T., and McGeachie, L. (2014). African drumming: A holistic approach to reducing stress and improving health? *Journal of Cardiovascular Medicine, 15*(6), 441–446. doi:410.2459/JCM.0000000000000046.

Smith, J. D. (2004). Playing like a girl: The queer laughter of the feminist improvising group. In *The other side of nowhere: Jazz, improvisation, and communities in dialogue*, edited by D. Fischlin and A. Heble, 224–243. Middletown, CT: Wesleyan University Press.

Smith, S. (2013). Complicated sublimity: Evan Parker interviewed. *The Quietus*. https://thequietus.com/articles/12819-evan-parker-interview.

Stensæth, K. (2017). *Responsiveness in music therapy improvisation. A perspective inspired by Mikhail Bakhtin*. New Bronfels, TX: Barcelona Publishers.

Sternberg, R. J. (2005). Creativity or creativities? *International Journal of Human-Computer Studies, 63*, 370–382.

Stevens, J., Doyle, J., and Cooke, O. (2007). *Search & reflect: A music workshop handbook*. London: Rockschool.

Sutton, J. (2002). The pause that follows: Silence, improvised music, and music therapy. *Nordic Journal of Music Therapy, 11*(1), 27–38.

Takeuchi, H., Sekiguchi, A., Taki, Y., Yokoyama, S., Yomogida, Y., Komuro, N., . . . Kawashima, R. et al. (2010). Training of working memory impacts structural connectivity. *The Journal of Neuroscience, 30*(9), 3297–3303. doi:10.1523/jneurosci.4611-09.2010.

Thaut, M.H. (2010) Neurologic Music Therapy in Cognitive Rehabilitation. *Music Perception: An Interdisciplinary Journal*, Vol. 27 No. 4, pp. 281-285.

Thomson, W. (2006) *Soundpainting: the art of live composition*. Workbook 1. New York, NY: Walter Thompson.

Toop, D. (2016). *Into the maelstrom: Music, improvisation, and the dream of freedom, before 1970*. London: Bloomsbury.

Trevarthen, C. (2002). Origins of musical identity: Evidence from infancy for musical social awareness. In *Musical identities*, edited by R. MacDonald, D. Miell, and D. Hargreaves, 21–38. Oxford: Oxford University Press.

Trondalen, G., and Bonde, L. O. (2012). Music therapy: Models and interventions. In *Music, health, and well-being*, edited by R. MacDonald, G. Kreutz, and L. Mijtchell, 40–64. New York: Oxford University Press.

Veblen, K. K. (2007). The many ways of community music. *International Journal of Community Music, 1*(1), 5–21. doi:10.1386/ijcm.1.1.5_1.

Virkkula, E. (2016). Informal in formal: The relationship of informal and formal learning in popular and jazz music master workshops in conservatoires. *International Journal of Music Education, 34*(2), 171–185. doi:10.1177/0255761415617924.

Weiss, J. (2006). *Steve Lacy: Conversations*. Durham, NC: Duke University Press.

Wetherell, M., and Edley, N. (1999). Negotiating hegemonic masculinity: Imaginary positions and psycho-discursive practices. *Feminism and Psychology, 9*, 333. doi:10.1177/0959353599009003012.

Whyte, I. B. (1985). *The crystal chain letters: Architectural fantasies by Bruno Taut and his circle*. Cambridge, MA: MIT Press.

Wigram, T. (2004). *Improvisation: Methods and techniques for music therapy clinicians, educators, and students*. London: Jessica Kingsley.

Wilson, G. B., and MacDonald, R. A. (2005). The meaning of the blues: Musical identities in talk about jazz. *Qualitative Research in Psychology, 2*(4), 341–363. doi:10.1191/1478088705qp044oa.

Wilson, G. B., and MacDonald, R. A. R. (2012). The sign of silence: Negotiating musical identities in an improvising ensemble. *Psychology of Music, 40*(5), 558–573. doi:10.1177/0305735612449506.

Wilson, G. B., and MacDonald, R. A. R. (2016). Musical choices during group free improvisation: A qualitative psychological investigation. *Psychology of Music, 44*(5), 1029–1043. doi:10.1177/0305735615606527.

Wilson, G. B., and MacDonald, R. A. R. (2017). The construction of meaning within free improvising groups: A qualitative psychological investigation. *Psychology of Aesthetics, Creativity, and the Arts, 11*(2), 136–146. doi:10.1037/aca0000075.

Wilson, G. B., and MacDonald, R. A. R. (2017). The ear of the beholder: Improvisation, ambiguity, and social contexts in the constructions of musical identities. In *The Oxford handbook of musical identities*, edited by R. MacDonald, D. Hargreaves, and D. Miell, 105–221. Oxford: Oxford University Press.

Wilson, G. B., and MacDonald, R. A. R. (2019). "It's got a life of its own": Teaching group improvisation through responsive choices. In *Expanding the space for improvisation*, edited by G. G. Johansen, K. M. Holdhus, C. Larsson, and U. MacGlone, 211–228. London: Routledge.

Winter, D. A., and Reed, N. (Eds.). (2016). *The Wiley handbook of personal construct psychology*. London: John Wiley & Sons.

Index

Tables and figures are indicated by *t* and *f* following the page number

For the benefit of digital users, indexed terms that span two pages (e.g., 52–53) may, on occasion, appear on only one of those pages.

www.ingramcontent.com/pod-product-compliance
Ingram Content Group UK Ltd.
Pitfield, Milton Keynes, MK11 3LW, UK
UKHW020226250726
13967UKWH00001B/221